TEN VICTORIAN POETS

TEN
VICTORIAN
POETS

―――――――――――――

BY
F. L. LUCAS

Fellow of King's College, Cambridge,
University Reader in English

―――――――――――――

ARCHON BOOKS
1966

First Edition (Eight Victorian Poets) 1930
Second Edition (Ten Victorian Poets) 1940
Third Edition   1948

Third edition reprinted 1966 by arrangement with
CAMBRIDGE UNIVERSITY PRESS
in an unaltered and unabridged edition

Library of Congress Catalog Card Number: 66-13343
Printed in the United States of America

To
JOHN HAYWARD

CONTENTS

INTRODUCTION

My thanks are due to the B.B.C. for permission to publish the talks that follow (except the chapters on W. Morris, Patmore, and Christina Rossetti), and to *Life and Letters* for leave to republish the criticism of Clough. Passages have been added here and there throughout the book; but naturally in a work of this size those who have a familiar knowledge of Victorian poetry can look for little new. My hope is rather, if possible, to do something to encourage a wider reading of that poetry by a wider public.

For the present age, I believe, reads too little poetry. A certain select minority indeed, led by its critical Scribes and Pharisees, does read only too much about it and about it: but that is no substitute. Yet we need it. It is not a luxury; it is something without which life remains one-eyed. Nor is it a preserve of the cultured; the greatest verse, from Sophocles to Shakespeare, from Homer to Hardy, has appealed to common humanity. It is like a hardening of the arteries in an ageing society, that poetry should to-day have so lost touch with the ordinary man, and the ordinary man with poetry.

For several centuries now the civilized races have been becoming more and more pre-occupied with this world to the exclusion of any other. The gods are twilit; the peoples of the grave grow ever ghostlier; for a large part of mankind the future life is a dead dream of the past. This tendency may, of course, be reversed; but I see no reason to suppose it. For the present, at all events, human beings give their minds more than ever before to material and ephemeral things. The priests have lost credit; the prophets are dumb; the philosophers still wrestle as of old with one another, lost to sight in their private clouds of dust; faster and faster mankind whirls away from them in the wake of the scientist, the real master of the modern world. But whither? To what end? The scientist, his eyes fixed on his own special problems of the moment, sees that no more clearly than anyone else. He and his kind have infinitely extended human power, infinitely lessened human pain; and yet? Who can sit by an English mainroad in normal years, watching that endless serpent of motor-cars gliding past the petrol-pumps that suckle it—those nurseries of red and yellow Robots that beset with their garish arrogance mile after mile of English country—and pronounce with carefree confidence the name of "Progress"? What fills the minds of this triumphal procession of charioteers? Science has equipped each of them with a magic engine such as the kings of the past would have given provinces to possess. And now what use do they make of it? What go they out to see? Perhaps for a moment in that long array the dreaming eye may discern the spectre of a distant age—the Roman noble of Lucretius driving desperately down the Appian Way, from town to country and from country back to town again, tortured two thousand years ago by the same feverish futility.

> No easier nor no quicker passed
> The impracticable hours.

Our age is not insensible to beauty—we go roaring out of our cities in pursuit of it; yet we nonchalantly allow tripper and builder to litter that beauty into desolation. Our age is not denuded of imagination—we crowd cinemas where every rag of common probability is left behind at the entrance; yet the visions we see there are merely commonplaces of cheap wish-fulfilment. The more crudely realistic our desires, the more unreal their satisfactions become. Science, in a word, has largely served to re-arm the barbarians. The Church was once, for the masses of the people, the stronghold of a certain culture; the Bible was a literature for them. Not now. Nor is there much comfort in the idea that the Church of the past may be replaced by the State of the future and that men may learn the ways of the ant only too well in perfectly ordered Termitecommunities, where the individual is endowed with every benefit except individuality. Shoulder to shoulder, the new Science and the old Attila loom above what civilization we possess.

It is not unusual, after drawing a dark picture of this sort and oppressing the helpless reader with its gloom, to display through a rift in the clouds some shining panacea. Poetry is not that. It has been at times a great civilizing influence; but it would be rash to expect very much of it in that way to-day. Our communities have grown too vast. What poetry can hope to do is to change, not the world at large, but, every here and there, some individual soul; to transform not the facts, but the face, of life; to provide for us an escape into illusion and the solace of a braver disillusion. It cannot give us a new Heaven and a new earth; but it can give us new eyes with which to see the old. At times that does almost as well. It would be insincere to claim too much. Existence affords intenser pleasures than poetry can ever give, intenser pains than poetry can cure. Yet it can always enrich the first and, in the long run, lighten the second; it can call in another world to redress the balance of this; it is a possession, not "for ever" (what have we to do with eternity?), but for life. It stays when other things fail us. "Of human existence", says Marcus Aurelius, "the time is a

point, and the substance a flux, and the perceptions
of the senses dim, and the fabric of the body subject
to corruption, and the soul a whirl, and fortune
incalculable, and fame capricious. In fine, the things
of the body are as a flowing river, and the things of
the soul as a vapour and a dream, and life but a
warfare and a stranger's sojourning, and after-fame
but oblivion. What then shall be our guide and
safeguard? One thing, and only one—Philosophy."
That austere conclusion some will accept; others,
whose heads incline less to this marble hardness of
the Stoic's creed than to Montaigne's "pillow of
doubt", may answer "Not Philosophy, but Poetry".
Stone pillows may bring beatific visions of Heaven
with whole ladderfuls of angels. But who knows if
they are real? Next morning only a stone and an
aching head remain. "Poetry", Socrates might have
said, knowing only that he knew nothing, "is a more
philosophical thing than Philosophy." For Poetry
knows that her visions may all be dreams; her true
value endures though they prove false. If she gives
her pleasure, then she gives her pleasure; she bids no
man believe her make-believe; she has no Thirty-nine
Articles; hard as the critics toil to provide legal bonds
for her, she slips through their fat fingers, fancy-free.

And yet how constant, on the other hand, as well
as keen, the pleasures of poetry can be, those little

guess who have never cultivated them, nor gone about haunted for days by some perfect snatch of music like—

> Sunt apud infernos tot milia formosarum,

or   Les violons vibrant derrière les collines,

or   Tell me not here, it needs not saying,
>   What tune the enchantress plays.

And so too with the eye and the imagination that poetry once has touched—the world for them will never at its worst be quite so drab and meaningless and "prosaic", as it can otherwise become. It is like the transfiguring power of sudden sunlight on the dullest landscape, of a perfect voice on the most commonplace of words.

"It's very rusty", said the old porter dolefully, fumbling all the while with the lock, that grated with an unpleasant sound but would not turn. "There's nothing else wrong with it, but it's terribly rusty. No one uses this gate now."

The words, ordinary enough in themselves, filled Genji with an unaccountable depression. How swiftly the locks rust, the hinges grow stiff, on doors that close behind us! "I am more than thirty", he thought; and it seemed to him impossible to go on doing things just as though they would last...as though people would remember..."And yet", he said to himself, "I know that even at this moment the sight of something very beautiful, were it only some common flower or tree, might in an instant make life again full of meaning and reality."

Those words were written in the Far East fifty years before Harold the Saxon fell on Senlac Hill; and yet how close they are to Keats, whose depressions the setting sun could always put to rights—or rather the poetic imagination he brought to bear on the setting sun! For to Coleridge, his poetic imagination once faded, no sunsets, we may remember, could be of any avail.

Or take another example, not from ancient Japan, but from modern France—Proust's picture of that worldly restaurant at Rivebelle, where his fancy suddenly transfigures the round tables into the planets of a mediaeval astronomy and the hurried waiters into other heavenly bodies wheeling on their courses.

Assises derrière un massif de fleurs, deux horribles caissières, occupées à des calculs sans fin, semblaient deux magiciennes occupées à prévoir par des calculs astrologiques les bouleversements qui pouvaient parfois se produire dans cette voûte céleste conçue selon la science du moyen âge. *Et je plaignais un peu tous les dîneurs parce que je sentais que pour eux les tables rondes n'étaient pas des planètes et qu'ils n'avaient pas pratiqué dans les choses un sectionnement qui nous débarrasse de leur apparence coutumière et nous permet d'apercevoir des analogies.* Ils pensaient qu'ils dînaient avec telle ou telle personne, que le repas coûterait à peu près tant, et qu'ils recommenceraient le lendemain.

The poetry of restaurants may not be of the highest order; but I have chosen this instance precisely because is shows how a poetic vision works even in restaurants. In the same way Hardy's sensitiveness to the unseen, his quick ear for the tiny whispering voices of the past, made him too prefer, in his own words, "the beauty of association to the beauty of aspect, and a beloved relative's old battered tankard to the finest Greek vase".

Given the greater abundance in the world of old battered tankards and even of beloved relatives than of the finest Greek vases, here the poet proves richer not only than the Philistine, but also than the aesthetic connoisseur. And a "poet" in this sense, every person of any imagination, even though he never writes a line of verse, can in some measure become. It is easier, as I have said, to find a new vision of the world than a new world; and it is wiser in a life where nothing lasts, to lay up what treasures we can outside the reach of space and time, to cultivate what pleasures we can, immune from change and circumstance. Poetry has kept the flames of Troy alight for ever—as bright for mankind to-day as three thousand years ago; as bright for each one of us to-day as yesterday, to-morrow as to-day, till all to-morrows cease for us.

> Where blooms the flower when her petals fade,
> Where sleepeth echo by earth's music made,
> Where all things transient to the changeless win,
> There waits the peace thy spirit dwelleth in.

Trite as it is, we can never remember vividly enough that nothing matters, ultimately, but good states of mind. It is hard to realize that Hardy, having Walter de la Mare's *Listeners* read to him on his death-bed, may even then have been more vividly and truly alive than most of us in our hours of stolid health. The modern man, indeed, regards as a piece of quaint eccentricity the story that tells how the ancient Syracusans thought liberty no extravagant reward for prisoners of war who could recite them new pieces of Euripides, the poet of their deadliest enemies. That was not at all our own attitude in the First World War to Wagner. Yet it might not occur to us that the ancients had a saner sense of values than our own? Certainly it is worth reflecting that a large part of the education of the most brilliant race in history consisted in learning poetry like Homer's by heart.

After all, one of the crucial problems of all civilized life, as Plato and Aristotle already saw, is what to do with the emotions that survive from man's un-civilized past. Violence ceases; hate and jealousy and rage have to be more and more repressed; the terror of imminent danger, the exultant reaction from danger dared and escaped, grow ever rarer. Only love is left. As its rivals dwindle, it towers aloft alone; until this one passion has become the obsession and the tyrant of modern life and literature. It is indeed the very crown of our existence; it stands between us and a desert of apathetic boredom; we are built to feel, and any person with a heart inevitably loathes and despises one without. Yet this one surviving universal passion is of its very nature transient, uncontrollable, at the mercy of circumstance. We cannot build our whole lives upon it. We must have other outlets for feeling, or burst, or turn into vegetables. And what outlets in fact we find! Cup-ties, rock-climbing, film-melodramas, detective-stories—with these we tickle towards a peaceful death by inanition those wild impulses that enabled our remote forefathers to preserve life and transmit it. It was here that Aristotle saw how the poet's imagination could provide the outlet that real life denies. Only he thought the outlet necessary lest the imprisoned emotions should explode; whereas to-day we surely need it rather lest they should perish of starvation. In literature we find the passions life withholds.

INTRODUCTION

We cannot voyage through magic seas like Odysseus; but we can read Homer still.

Yet, after all, poetry is not simply a substitute for the imperfectness of actual experience. Indeed it can only partly replace it. For those who live too much in books, even books are dead. By that danger Swinburne perished; and that danger Milton foresaw when he demanded that the poet's own life should itself be "a true poem". Ultimately, life and poetry are interlocked. For there is no commentator like life; we realize sometimes with amazement how little in our nonage we sounded the real depth of seemingly transparent passages in literature. And on the other hand, there are moments in life when the transience and sadness of existence are made bearable only by their poetry; there are people in the world, a few, who carry into the art of living, consciously or not, a certain grace, a certain fineness, a certain sense of style, which redeems them from the sterile futility of most human struggling. They suffer, they grow old, they are forgotten; but they were never ugly, nor squalid, nor ridiculous. If anything can justify the world, it is its beauty; and they were part of that. There are a great many actions that would never be committed if men could always remember poetry.

The difficulty, for some reason, is to read it. There

are so many easier things to read—books about poetry among them. A hundred people will finish a new book on Tennyson for one who explores *In Memoriam*; the modern reader has lost all sense of reality. Yet it is clearly futile to go on sitting at the mountain's foot listening for ever to other men's descriptions of the view from its cloven peak. A few hints of the way may indeed help; there are pitfalls to avoid, deserts to skirt, particular beauties not to miss. But it is not without misgiving that I have added yet one more to the number of guides; and it would be far better for the reader to shut this book at once than to let it curtail at all the time he needs for a proper reading of the Victorian Poets themselves.

NOTE TO THIRD EDITION

A few verbal changes have been made; a few points corrected (for example, it is now proved that the attack on Tennyson in the *Quarterly* for April 1833 was not by Lockhart, but by J. W. Croker); and the Selected Bibliography brought up to date.

I

TENNYSON

Ni trop haut, ni trop bas, c'est le souverain style:
Tel fut celui d'Homère et celui de Virgile.

RONSARD.

In a wooded hollow in Lincolnshire a dark-haired mournful little boy is carving a sandstone-rock. One by one from under his penknife appear the three words—BYRON IS DEAD. For him, as for half England, with that message from Missolonghi, the light of the world seems darkened. / And, indeed, a real darkness has fallen on English poetry. For three years now Keats has lain at rest in the Protestant cemetery at Rome; and Shelley for two beside him. Wordsworth and Coleridge survive only as pale ghosts of themselves. And who else is left? Not for eighteen years yet was the world to begin to realize that in this gipsy-faced boy had arisen their successor in the long line of English poets—Alfred Tennyson. But that day is still far off; and meanwhile the boy is growing into a wayward, handsome, contradictory youth, with a magnificent sculptured face and a great mane of black hair. His poetry begins early. A play called *The Devil and the Lady*, written at fourteen and printed in 1930, shows both a spontaneous gaiety and delight in character which the later Tennyson might well have envied, and a command of blank verse, of which he need not have been ashamed at any age:

There is a clock in Pandemonium,
Hard by the burning throne of my great grandsire,
The slow vibrations of whose pendulum
With click-clack alternation to and fro
Sound "Ever, Never" thro' the courts of Hell.

At seventeen he breaks into print, together with Charles Tennyson, in the very juvenile *Poems by Two Brothers* (1826). Before he has been long at Cambridge, the most brilliant group of his fellow-undergraduates has already hailed in him not only the poet, but the poet-philosopher of the coming age. Fortunate young man! And yet all is not sunshine. Like his father, the rector of Somersby, he has terrible fits of melancholy; in the words of an unusually self-revealing poem, written later but excluded from the *Collected Works*—

> Immeasurable sadness!
> And I know it as a poet,
> And I meet it and I greet it,
> Immeasurable sadness!
> And the voice that apes a nation—
> Let it cry "An affectation",
> Or "A fancy", or "A madness",
> But I know it as a poet,
> And I meet it and I greet it,
> And I say it and repeat it,
> Immeasurable sadness!

Stranger still, this youth who looks like a life-guardsman has more than a touch of schoolgirl about him; he is morbidly shy; he writes poems with titles like *The Skipping-rope* and *The Darling Room*; and when he reads his work to his friends, it is understood that there must be no word of criticism.

4

Still, the poetry is there. In 1830, when he is twenty-one, appears a new volume.

> At eve the beetle boometh
>   Athwart the thicket lone:
> At noon the wild bee hummeth
>   About the moss'd headstone:
> At midnight the moon cometh,
>   And looketh down alone.

Here, for those with ears, was a new note in English poetry. Some heard it. Coleridge at Highgate might solemnly pronounce that the author of this volume did not "very well understand what metre was"; so prone are the greatest critics, even, to nod and slide heavily under the table. But though Coleridge might show that he did not himself always very well understand what poetry was, others praised the book and it was followed by a successor in 1832. But now the world went suddenly black for Tennyson. The new volume, though it contained work of his very best, like *The Lotos-Eaters* and *The Lady of Shalott*, was roughly handled, as the work of a namby-pamby, niminy-piminy poet, in the *Quarterly Review* by Croker; who, unrepentantly recalling his attack on *Endymion* fifteen years before, now sneered at Tennyson as "a new prodigy of genius—another and brighter star in that galaxy or *milky way* of poetry of which the lamented Keats was the harbinger". To-day we can appreciate Croker's irony more fully even than he intended; but in 1833 the *Quarterly* still wielded an influence such as modern critics, fortunately, do not possess even in their wildest dreams. It was like being trodden on by an elephant. There was a roar of public ridicule; and Tennyson shrank back into his shell for a whole ten years of silence. But far worse followed. In September 1833 Arthur Hallam, the person who meant most in the world to Tennyson, died suddenly at Vienna. By that loss we have gained *In Memoriam, The Two Voices, Break, break, break,* and *Ulysses*; we cannot know what it cost Tennyson. Years passed. From the poet's chimney silently ascended an endless sacrificial smoke of tobacco and burning poetry. Then he fell in love with Emily Sellwood; but for one so poor marriage seemed impossible. Little wonder if his black fits at times almost overwhelmed him. But at last, in 1842, he was persuaded to publish again. And now fortune began to turn. He lost, indeed, a great part of his small capital in a typically Victorian scheme for making carved oak by machinery. But his reputation had been silently growing; he was praised by Edgar Allan Poe in 1844 as "the noblest poet that ever lived" and, more moderately, by Wordsworth in 1845 as "decidedly the first of our living poets"; he was given a pension on the Civil

6

List; and in 1850, the year of *In Memoriam*, largely by
the influence of Prince Albert he became Poet
Laureate; he became too, at last, the husband of
Emily Sellwood. His good fortune was complete;
even the cake and the dresses contrived to arrive late
for the wedding; which made it, said he, "the nicest
wedding I was ever at".

This central year of the century is also the central
point in Tennyson's career. Forty-one years lay
behind him; forty-two remained. Henceforth his
life slopes smoothly downhill; and so perhaps does
his poetry—though with magnificent recoveries.
The Idylls of the King and *Enoch Arden* lodged him
securely in the vast bosom of the British public; he
bought Farringford, then Aldworth; he was raised to
the peerage; he became to Queen Victoria in poetry
almost what Disraeli was in politics; he became to
her subjects lion and unicorn in one, the national
poet of England as no living man had ever been—not
Chaucer, nor Shakespeare, nor Milton, nor Wordsworth. And so this imposing figure who looked,
said Dobell, as if he could have written Homer's
Iliad itself, played his part with dignity up to that
crowning moment in 1892 when the full October
moon looked down through the tall oriel at Aldworth
on the white features of the Laureate of the Empire,
as he lay dying with Shakespeare clasped in his

stiffening hand. Not his own King Arthur passed
with more stateliness out of the world of living men.

And yet, after all, what sort of human being was
there hidden under the laurel-wreath he wore so
well? The usual bundle of human contradictions.
Imagine a proud leonine figure, romantically awe-
inspiring in his dark mantle, and yet so shy as to flee
from the sheep his short sight mistook for lion-
hunting tourists; now gruffly replying to an effusive
lady who begged at parting to know what she could
do for him, "Anything, except kiss me in front of the
cabman", now indulgently burgling his own larder
to find his dog chicken-bones; or again, with a
mixture of both qualities, exclaiming in affectionate
irritation at his mother's readiness to weep on every
possible and impossible occasion—"Damn your eyes,
mother!"; a man who seems half bear as he sits,
dark and shaggy, over his clay pipe and public-
house port, or growls, "I like my meat in wedges",
and yet the author of such lollipoppery as *The
May Queen*, sneered at by Bulwer Lytton as "School-
miss Alfred"; a humourist who would read aloud
St Simeon Stylites shaking with laughter, and yet
could write without a smile that extraordinary
description of an Arthurian moustache as "the
knightly growth that fringed his lips"; a character
whose Johnsonian good sense made Thackeray say

TENNYSON

"Tennyson is the wisest man I know", yet whose poetry seemed to Matthew Arnold intellectually second-rate; a lover of science who yet dreaded its conclusions; a victim of "immeasurable sadness", talking to Rogers about death "till the tears ran down their faces", and growled at by Carlyle for "sitting on a dung-heap brooding over innumerable dead dogs", yet still clinging to optimism with the courage, not of faith, but of despair; and finally a poet lofty and aloof as his own eagle perched above the world, who yet screamed with agony at the first nip of the tiniest critic. Mr Harold Nicolson in his admirable biography relates one crowning anecdote of this, which at least deserves to be true—how after dinner at Balliol Tennyson read some of his latest work, not quite up to his best standard. When he ceased, there was a long silence, broken by the chirping treble of Jowett, "If I were you, Tennyson, I wouldn't publish those". There was a yet more awful hush; and then the booming bass of the outraged poet, "If it comes to that, Master, the sherry you gave us at luncheon to-day was positively filthy".

All this is not the Victorian vision of the Poet Laureate; but if the portrait is less reverential, is it really less likeable? Human beings are, after all, more attractive than idols; a halo only obscures a living face. Surely it is a relief under the Bard to find a man. But a poet?—was he truly that? For since that October moon sank over Aldworth half a century ago, a mist has slowly risen and covered like a shroud the memory of Tennyson. His resurrection has often been prophesied: it has hardly come. Is he to be lastingly canonized among the sacred names of English poetry, or no? Let us first hear the Devil's Advocate. What are the charges against him?

First, that he was intellectually timid, a prophet of comfortable things, a priest without a real faith, a philosopher who could not reason, a political thinker who trimmed over the problems of poverty and turned the Woman's Question into a picnic.

> Then the maiden Aunt
> Took this fair day for text, and from it preach'd
> An universal culture for the crowd,
> And all things great.

Alas for that maiden Aunt—she has a regrettably large share in the works of Tennyson. And then the Devil's Advocate will doubtless quote also that brilliantly unkind parody by St John Hankin:

> When pondering much of how and why
>   And lost in philosophic lore,
>   The thought that two and two are four
> Consoles me in my agony.

TENNYSON

The sun sinks ever in the west,
And ever rises in the east.
I feel that this is sure at least,
And cannot doubt but it is best.

"Tennyson", says Matthew Arnold, in that
relentless, even voice of his, "with all his temperament
and artistic skill, is deficient in intellectual power."
Certainly Tennyson's descriptions of intellectual
processes are apt to be curious:

He fought his doubts and gathered strength,
He would not make his judgment blind—

did it never occur to the poet that the second line
might seem strangely in contradiction with the first?
In a word, Tennyson preached too much, without
well knowing what to say; and the surplice he dressed
his Muse in finally proved her winding-sheet.

Secondly, the charge will run, just as he could not
think deeply, he could not feel deeply either. He has
no passion, only pathos. *Elaine* or *Oenone* is pathetic,
not tragic: *Maud* shrieks when it tries to thunder.
"Tears, idle tears, I know not what they mean"—
precisely, cries the Devil's Advocate, Tennyson
did not know; but Byron knew, and the tears of
Baudelaire were never "idle".

Ange plein de bonté, connaissez-vous la haine,
Les poings crispés dans l'ombre, et les larmes de fiel,
Quand la Vengeance bat son infernal rappel,

Et de nos facultés se fait le capitaine?
Ange plein de bonté, connaissez-vous la haine?

Ange plein de beauté, connaissez-vous les rides,
Et la peur de vieillir, et ce hideux tourment
De lire la secrète horreur du devoûment
Dans les yeux où longtemps burent nos yeux avides?
Ange plein de beauté, connaissez-vous les rides?

Might not those bitter lines have been directly addressed by the French poet to the gentle Muse of his English contemporary?

Thirdly, it will be said, Tennyson cannot create character. His plays, for all the labour they cost him, are long dead and buried now. Nor can Lady Clara Vere de Vere or the Lord of Burleigh pretend to be still very lively; they feel their age, poor things.

Nor, fourthly, continues the Denying Spirit, is Tennyson a master of long narrative either, like William Morris. The *Idylls of the King* have no epic quality; their very name betrays them—Malory made into "Idylls"!—the spear of Malory's Lancelot twisted into a china shepherd's crook! Where the action of the story should hurry the reader on, Tennyson's style with its slow, over-polished perfectness is always holding him back, always crying, "Stay a moment; I am so beautiful". And as a picture of the real savagery of the Middle Ages, the *Idylls of the King* are about as adequate as a fancy-dress ball or a parish pageant. "We read at first Tennyson's *Idylls*", writes Carlyle to Emerson, "with profound recognition of the finely elaborated execution, and also of the inward perfection of vacancy and, to say truth, with considerable impatience at being treated so very like infants, though the lollipops were so superlative." And again comes that suave voice of Arnold's, with its stern summing-up: "I do not think Tennyson a great and powerful spirit in any line, as Goethe was in the line of thought, Wordsworth in that of contemplation, Byron, even, in that of passion". In short, this highly coloured fowl which the Victorians thought a Bird of Paradise, turns out after all to have been only a parrot.

That is what the Devil's Advocate says nowadays, when he has troubled to read Tennyson at all; or even when he has not. And what is the answer? The answer is, I think, that the Devil's evidence contains much truth; but not the whole truth; and in fact does not prove his case. Tennyson still remains a great poet, even though he may not have been a great thinker, nor a master of passion, nor of character, nor of long narrative. For he has other gifts, supreme gifts, of eye and ear and tongue. He is a great landscape-painter, and a great musician. He wrote many bad things, calculated to please his own age and now perished with it—so, for that matter, did Shakespeare. But he had style; and style, though it may not at once win the day for a poet, can win him eternity. Tennyson is the poet of the perfect phrase. He could make moments immortal— a sudden gleam of sun, a gust of wind in the forest, the white breaking of a wave; it is these that in return will give him immortality. From the first humming of that lonely bee above the grave of Claribel to the last great tide that in *Crossing the Bar* goes sweeping back into the seaward gloom, there is hardly a sound or colour in Nature that he has not fixed in perfect words for ever. He can tell stories too, as in *The Revenge* or *Maeldune*; he can express, if not passion, at least a Virgilian majesty of sadness for the world; he can even at moments be passionate, as in those stanzas the first of which Meredith's wife, dying alone and broken-hearted, asked in vain to have carved upon her tomb:

Come not, when I am dead,
　To drop thy foolish tears upon my grave,
To trample round my fallen head,
　And vex the unhappy dust thou wouldst not save.
There let the wind sweep and the plover cry;
　　But thou, go by.

Child, if it were thine error or thy crime
　I care no longer, being all unblest:
Wed whom thou wilt, but I am sick of Time,
　And I desire to rest.

14

TENNYSON

Pass on, weak heart, and leave me where I lie:
   Go by, go by.

Yet his strength lies elsewhere. As in some Italian
pictures, so with his, the human figures, however
lovely sometimes, are less perfect than the blue romantic wonder, the magic sadness, of the beckoning
world behind. The background crowns the work.
Claribel is forgotten for the bee and the beetle that
hum above her mossed headstone. Who was she?
We neither know nor care. It is not Mariana we
remember, but the far lowing of the oxen in the fen,
the drone of summer flies, the poplar shadow in the
low moonlight, the cold winds of dawn about the
Moated Grange. The heroine is indeed hardly more
a human figure than is the bird in *The Dying Swan*;
whose death, in its turn, is scarcely felt except as an
occasion for calling up one of Tennyson's most
living landscapes:

> The plain was grassy, wild and bare,
> Wide, wild, and open to the air,
> Which had built up everywhere
>   An under-roof of doleful gray.
> With an inner voice the river ran,
> Adown it floated a dying swan,
>   And loudly did lament.
>   It was the middle of the day.
> Ever the weary wind went on,
>   And took the reed-tops as it went.

In the same way Oenone's is only a painted grief upon a painted mountain; and yet what painting! Oenone herself is a true daughter of Tennyson: she too seems almost to sorrow less for her lost lover than for the mountain-pines he felled to fetch her rival from beyond the sea—

> They came, they cut away my tallest pines,
> My tall dark pines, that plumed the craggy ledge
> High over the blue gorge, and all between
> The snowy peak and snow-white cataract
> Foster'd the callow eaglet....Never, never more
> Shall lone Oenone see the morning mist
> Sweep thro' them; never see them overlaid
> With narrow moon-lit slips of silver cloud,
> Between the loud stream and the trembling stars.

Even the memory of her love calls up to her vision, not her lover's lips, but yet another landscape—

> kisses, thick as Autumn rains
> Flash in the pools of whirling Simois.

So too the agony of *Love and Duty*, the misery of *Tithonus* both fade and pass like paling stars into the splendours of a Tennysonian dawn, before those steeds of the morning that arise

And shake the darkness from their loosen'd manes,
And beat the twilight into flakes of fire.

Tennyson indeed hears not so much men, as trees talking—"the dry-tongued laurels' pattering talk", "the poplar's noise of falling showers", the dawn wind in the sycamore, the chestnut pattering earthward through the faded leaves. And he sees not only the trees, but every leaf upon them—the black ash-bud, the "million emeralds breaking from the ruby-budded lime". And again he can be vast as well as minute. No writer of our race, not even Swinburne, has so ruled the sea. If you ask whether this man was indeed a poet, make yourself an anthology of his seascapes alone. The Greeks fabled that Proteus, the Old Man of the Sea, to be won must be held through a hundred changing shapes. That is what Tennyson has done as none before or since; seizing alike its storm and calm, its wilder waves that smoke wind-whipped across the desolate North Sea, or "roar rock-thwarted under bellowing caves", and again that quieter swell which goes groping blindly on dull days up its long sea-hall in the caverns of the cliff, or shines reflected glassy-white in the wet sand as it breaks or, breaking, thins out and out to nothing across moon-marbled shores. As final examples, let suffice these two companion pictures of the Cornish sea; first, at the Coming of Arthur, before the taint of Guinevere—

> There
> All down the lonely coast of Lyonnesse,
> Each with a beacon-star upon his head,

And with a wild sea-light about his feet,
He saw them—headland after headland flame
Far on into the rich heart of the west:
And in the light the white mermaiden swam,
And strong man-breasted things stood from the sea,
And sent a deep sea-voice thro' all the land,
To which the little elves of chasm and cleft
Made answer, sounding like a distant horn;

and then at Arthur's Passing, after the last battle
with Modred on the mist-bound western strand—

                Only the wan wave
Brake in among dead faces, to and fro
Swaying the helpless hands, and up and down
Tumbling the hollow helmets of the fallen,
And shiver'd brands that once had fought with Rome,
And rolling far along the gloomy shores
The voice of days of old and days to be.

It was fitting that Tennyson's poetry should close
as it did, with that last tide, "too full for sound or
foam", which bore the old poet himself out into the
darkness where no harbours are.

When a man can do so much, is it not a little
graceless to ask more? "Poetry", said Matthew
Arnold, "should be criticism of life"; it is the sort of
thing critics say; and no great harm comes of it,
until poets start believing them. Poetry may criticize
life; or it may simply paint it, "making", in Sir
Philip Sidney's phrase, "the much-loved earth more

lovely". Who looks for problem-pictures from Raphael? Tennyson wasted only too much of himself in "criticism of life"; the gleam he followed was too often a wandering fire; but "though much is taken, much abides". There is no harm in laughing at the Victorians, provided we laugh also at ourselves; for if we do not, we shall, depend upon it, seem more ridiculous still to our own posterity. But after the laughter, there is room, still more, for silent wonder at this master who, coming so late in our literature, yet made such music, never heard before, and now surely to be heard through centuries, from the English country and the English tongue—

Lord over Nature, Lord of the visible earth,
Lord of the senses five.

II

BROWNING

Napoléon, les bras croisés, est plus expressif que l'Hercule furieux battant l'air de ses poings d'athlète. Jamais les gens passionnés ne sentiront cela . . . L'art de passion est sûr de plaire, mais ce n'est pas l'art souverain; il est vrai que l'époque démocratique rend peu à peu impossible l'art de sérénité: le troupeau turbulent ne connaît plus les dieux.

AMIEL.

At first sight those Great Twin Brethren of the Victorian era, Tennyson and Browning, are wildly unlike. What greater contrast could there be than between a tall black-cloaked, black-bearded, black-blooded recluse in the Isle of Wight, and a sociable frisking little gentleman, who drew from Tennyson the growl that Browning would certainly "die in a white tie", and from a lady who had met him at dinner the question—"Who was that too exuberant financier?"; between a poet whose style was as meticulously polished as he was himself shaggy and unkempt, and a poet who might wear evening-dress himself, but often left his hastily scribbled poems as fuzzy and prickly and tangled as a furze-bush; between the writer of *Tithonus*, with an immeasurable sadness underlying his talk about "the larger hope", and the writer of *Rabbi Ben Ezra*, who looked on the world and, behold, it was very good, with an even better one to follow? They are as different as the lady in the Japanese story, who kept butterflies, from her neighbour, the lady who preferred creeping things and caterpillars. The contrast had already struck contemporaries. FitzGerald found in Tennyson unforgettable things, in Browning only "Cockney sublime, Cockney energy": Carlyle wrote, "Alfred knows how to jingle, Browning does not", and again of Browning, "I wish he had taken to prose. Browning has far more ideas than Tennyson, but is not so truthful. Tennyson means what he says, poor fellow. Browning has a meaning in his twisted sentences, but he does not really go into anything or believe much about it. He accepts conventional values".

Here Carlyle seems to me, though he exaggerates Browning's inability to "jingle", to be mainly right. But under this contrast between the two poets there lies, I think, a deeper resemblance. They were both typically Victorian. Browning tended to wear his Victorian clothes inside out, by way of being original; but they were the same clothes; and now that time has worn them thin, Browning too looks a little threadbare. Both he and Tennyson seem to me pure poets damaged by being too much honoured as prophets in their own country. In consequence they were led more and more to preach, where they should have sung. The mantle of Elijah was thrown upon them: under it they lost their vision and their heads. Donne was wiser, who wrote lyrics in his youth and sermons in his old age; and so, instead of muddling the two, made great literature of both.

Still, when we regret that the Victorian poets should have spent so much of their force on propaganda, there is one point we tend to forget. This conviction of their own importance as thinkers and teachers may have helped them as well as hindered; if it led them to believe in much nonsense, it may also have helped them to believe in themselves, and so to accomplish much that "we half-believers in our casual creeds" cannot. For though our generation can criticize the Victorian poets, let us frankly admit that it cannot equal them. Even a flimsy banner may be better to fight under than none at all.

But as we look back to-day on Browning's life and work, both alike seem to me to gain a sudden interest at the point where he turns from a rather childish philosopher into a passionate human being. His early years had lacked colour: he grew up in a comfortable, uneventful home in Camberwell and, when his father said, "Well, Robert, what are you going to be?", Robert had only to reply that he thought he would be a poet, and sit down to prepare himself for that vocation by reading through Johnson's *Dictionary*. Then in 1845, when he was three and thirty and might have complained with much more justice than Byron at that age,

> What has life, then, brought to me?
> Nothing except thirty-three,

something happened. He suddenly took pen and wrote to a completely strange lady: "I love your books, dear Miss Barrett, and I love you too".

There is no need to recall that mid-Victorian love-story, as moving as Rossetti's or Meredith's, which still forms the subject of a new book once every six months—the pale little poetess, Elizabeth Barrett, with her black, spaniel ringlets, shuttered up in a darkened room in Wimpole Street; that terrible patriarch her father, with his West Indian slaves and his mansion in Herefordshire built so appropriately in the Turkish style, whose first and last commandment to his sons and daughters was, "Thou shalt not marry", and whose transports of fury at the mere mention of an engagement used to leave the miserable culprit swooning in the arms of her half-swooning sisters; and then the gradual miracle by which the supposed hopeless invalid was fascinated by her lover into that audacious flight to Italy. "So", commented Wordsworth, "Robert Browning and Miss Barrett have gone off together. I hope they understand each other; no one else would." They did—with a completeness few married couples have ever equalled. Mr Barrett's comments are not recorded; but he never forgave his daughter, never condescended to open her letters though, in the state of her health, for all he knew they might have contained the news that she was dying. His children had judged him only too well; as Elizabeth put it: "'If a prince from Eldorado should come with a pedigree of lineal descent from some signiory in the moon in one hand, and a ticket of good behaviour from the nearest Independent Chapel in the other....' 'Why even then', said my sister Arabella, 'it would not do'". To explain Mr Barrett, indeed, it needed Dr Freud.

But after this one burst of romance Browning's life settled down again into that even tenour which it kept till its end at Venice in 1889. And so the year 1845 remains almost as central in his career as 1850 in Tennyson's. It produced what seems to me one of his best single volumes, *Dramatic Romances*; it produced his own romance with Elizabeth Barrett: the memorial of which, in its turn, is his most famous work, *The Ring and the Book*. For Browning would never have written that with such passion, had he not seen in the frail little Pompilia his own dead wife, and in her rescue by the priest Caponsacchi a counterpart of that elopement from Wimpole Street more than twenty years before.

And so it is, I think, the Browning who feels, that matters; not the Browning who speculates about the Universe. For his speculations were rather a South Sea Bubble, however brightly coloured. But just as Tennyson outlives his own prophecies, as a painter of sky and earth, a musician of wave and tree, so Browning becomes worth hearing when he turns from his preaching to catch the leap of a lover's pulse

or the answering flush on a girl's face. It is his
lovers that live, just as the loves of Horace have
outlived all the laws of Augustus,—happy or tragic,
faithful or faithless; triumphant in their brief pride
above the dust of a dead city, while the sheep-bells
tinkle where its belfries tolled, or saddened amid the
desolate indifference of the Roman Campagna, or
stepping gaily from a gondola in Venice to meet
the dagger gleaming in the archway's gloom; now
watching the alchemist pound the blue poison for a
rival's lips, or quietly strangling a fickle mistress, so
as to keep her always, with her own coiling hair; now
pressing a geranium-leaf for remembrance in a dead
girl's hand, or riding for the last time on earth with a
woman loved in vain, or remembering sadly, yet
gladly, on a death-bed the stolen meetings of long ago.
The same fine vitality breathes in Browning's
treatment of other sides of human life, whenever
there is no ill-pointed moral being dug into the
reader's ribs—when the Duke of Ferrara describes
his last Duchess, or Caliban sits creating his god
Setebos in his own image, or Childe Roland comes to
the cursed Tower among the sunset hills. Where
Browning is content to be a pure artist, he can be a
vivid one. Of course the Browning Societies with
typical English Philistinism wanted a moral even for
Childe Roland; an adulterous generation asking for a

sign, they approached the author; but for once
they had to go empty away. It was just a dream-
fantasy made from a phrase in Shakespeare, a horse
in a tapestry, a tower seen in the Carrara Mountains—
he forgot the rest. But perhaps of all these characters
the most brilliant is the Bishop who orders his
tomb at St Praxed's, with his naïve and nonchalant
Renaissance way of serving at once Jove and Jehovah,
Aphrodite and Mary of Nazareth. Most of Browning's
figures are very much himself; he stands in their
shoes rather than in their skins; in consequence, as a
dramatist, he is no Shakespeare: but when, as here,
the character required does fit his own personality
and his own tastes, the result can be astonishingly
effective. Here, his moral disapproval for the nonce
suspended, Browning with his appreciation of the
good things of both worlds could feel a vivid, if
ironic, sympathy towards his half-pagan church-
man—

And then how I shall lie through centuries,
And hear the blessed mutter of the mass,
And see God made and eaten all day long,
And feel the steady candle-flame, and taste
Good strong thick stupefying incense-smoke!
For as I lie here, hours of the dead night,
Dying in state and by such slow degrees,
I fold my arms as if they clasped a crook,
And stretch my feet forth straight as stone can point,

And let the bedclothes for a mortcloth drop
Into great laps and folds of sculptor's-work:
And as yon tapers dwindle, and strange thoughts
Grow, with a certain humming in my ears,
About the life before I lived this life,
And this life too, popes, cardinals, and priests,
St Praxed at his sermon on the mount,
Your tall pale mother with her talking eyes,
And new-found agate urns as fresh as day,
And marble's language, Latin pure, discreet,
—Aha, ELUCESCEBAT quoth our friend?
No Tully, said I, Ulpian at the best!
Evil and brief hath been my pilgrimage.
All *lapis*, all, sons! Else I give the Pope
My villas! Will ye ever eat my heart?
Ever your eyes were as a lizard's, quick,
They glitter like your mother's for my soul....

To paint men's ways, then, not to justify God's, seems to me Browning's business, would he but have minded it. Here, indeed, he provides another interesting contrast with Tennyson. For in Tennyson, as we have seen, the human figures matter less than the landscape, the Moated Grange moves us more than Mariana herself, many-fountained Ida than Oenone's tears: but in Browning the exact reverse is true—the world of nature matters less to him than human beings. It forms only the background of his portraits; indeed it often becomes itself half-humanized. His hills lie like giants watching a hunted

beast at bay, their chins upon their hands; his trees
cluster round a lake as wild men round a sleeping girl,
or gaze at the sun setting in the cloudy west, as a girl
after her lover; his forests for an instant relax their
ancient aloofness to make two human beings one:

A moment after, and *hands unseen*
  Were hanging the night around us fast;
But we knew that a bar was broken between
  Life and life: we were mixed at last
In spite of the mortal screen.

The forests had done it; there they stood;
  We had caught for a moment the powers at play:
They had mingled us so, for once and good,
  Their work was done—we might go or stay,
They relapsed to their ancient mood.

   This difference provides an amusing contrast
between the two poets; but why, then, does Browning
seem inferior to Tennyson? The answer lies, I feel,
partly in his style, and partly in his personality. Both
writers were overfond of pointing morals; but
Tennyson did at least try also to adorn his tales.
He had an artistic conscience; too often Browning
had not. Listen:

> Never any more,
>   While I live,
> Need I hope to see his face
>   As before.

Once his love grown chill,
　　Mine may strive:
Bitterly we re-embrace,
　　Single still.

Was it something said,
　　Something done,
Vexed him? was it touch of hand,
　　Turn of head?
Strange! that very way
　　Love begun:
I as little understand
　　Love's decay.

Or again:

No protesting, dearest!
　　Hardly kisses even!
　　　Don't we both know how it ends?
How the greenest leaf turns serest,
　　Bluest outbreak—blankest heaven,
　　　Lovers—friends?...

Where we plan our dwelling
　　Glooms a graveyard surely!
　　　Headstone, footstone moss may drape,—
Name, date, violets hide from spelling,—
　　But, though corpses rot obscurely,
　　　Ghosts escape.

Ghosts! O breathing Beauty,
　　Give my frank word pardon!
　　　What if I—somehow, somewhere—
Pledged my soul to endless duty
　　Many a time and oft? Be hard on
　　　Love—laid there?

BROWNING

"What is wrong with the music of that?" you say.
Precisely, nothing: but what devil, then, could lead
a man with this lyric gift to write such things as—

Nor soul helps flesh more now than flesh helps soul,

where the consonants writhe in spitting heaps; or
to pile up the vulgarity of—

Go get you manned by Manning, and new-manned
By Newman, and mayhap wise-manned to boot
By Wiseman, and we'll see or else we won't!

Dr Jekyll was not more different from Mr Hyde than
the Browning who sings, from the Browning who
roars. Why, why did he do it? It was partly sheer
slovenliness; a man who could write a poem of
fifty pages in double columns within seven weeks, and
then print it from the first draft, leaving the punctua-
tion to be corrected by a French friend, had the
conscience of a pavement-artist. Secondly, Browning
had also a natural impediment of thought which
made it hard for him to construct even an intelligible
telegram. He did not put himself in his reader's
place, nor realize how difficult he was being. Of
Sordello, that monument of obscurity, the reading of
which after an illness reduced Douglas Jerrold to
tears under the impression that he must really have
lost his reason, Browning remarked to a friend that
he had produced something "clear at last". Similarly

even his love-letters to Elizabeth Barrett lose themselves in whirls of incoherence; and she had great difficulty in persuading him to explain to the public what he meant by his cryptic *Bells and Pomegranates*. This tendency was made worse by that Gothic love of the grotesque found also in other works contemporary with Browning's youth, such as *Pickwick* and *Sartor Resartus*. He is indeed one of those writers who treat language not as a musical instrument, needing delicacy no less than power in its handling, but rather as an iron bar which they are to twist and tangle in an exhibition of their prowess as professional strong men. As he himself says of his Sordello:

> He left imagining to try the stuff
> That held the imaged thing, and—let it writhe
> Never so fiercely—scarcely allowed a tithe
> To reach the light—his language.

But there was also an element of affectation in this negligence, a suggestion that such an intellectual giant as Robert Browning was above mere airs and graces. "In my youth", he says in one of his letters, "I wrote only musically, and after stopped all that so effectually that I now catch myself grudging my men and women their half-pound, like a parish-overseer the bread-dole of his charge." But why? There is a certain pose about that. So Plato said he saw the

BROWNING

pride of Antisthenes the Cynic peeping through the
holes in his rags. It is indeed as if the curse of
Browning's Paracelsus, a similar mixture of true poet
and charlatan, had fallen on Browning himself:

> I cannot feed on beauty for the sake
> Of beauty only, nor can drink in balm
> From lovely objects for their loveliness...
> I still must hoard and heap and class all truths
> With one ulterior purpose: I must know!

No doubt it succeeded for a time. It enabled
persons who liked puzzles to suppose they liked
poetry, and persons afraid of real thinking, to fancy
themselves intellectual. And the thicker the incense
rose from the Browning Societies, the more ragged
and rugged his style became. It paid Browning then:
since then it is Browning who pays. As Dryden said
of Cowley: "One of our late great poets is sunk in
his reputation because he could never forego any
conceit which came in his way, but swept like a drag-
net great and small."

But this unpleasant element in his style has, I
think, roots that go deeper down to an unpleasant
element in Browning's personality. Extremely vital,
he was also a little vulgar—with that assertiveness of
the self-made man who thinks to brazen out lack of
breeding by lack of manners. "He flourished about",
said Tennyson. It was true. And again was all that

masquerading as bishop or physician, woman or monster, which makes his works like some vast fancy-dress ball, partly an escape, one sometimes wonders, from seeing his own image too clearly in the glass? Was all that stamping and shouting half intended to drown a small voice that might have whispered in the ear of Dr Pangloss less comfortable things? It is strange how persistent character can be: Tennyson's first childish verse was, "I hear a voice that's speaking in the wind"; Browning's,

> Good people all, who wish to see
> A boy take physic, look at me.

The little Tennyson listens: the little Browning demands to be looked at. Turn to the farewell poems of their old age, *Crossing the Bar* and *Epilogue*: the same characteristics are still there. The old Tennyson listens to the soundless funeral-march of the outward sweeping tide; Browning calls the theatre of the world to take note how a Browning can live and die—

> One who never turned his back, but marched breast
>   forward,
>   Never doubted clouds would break,
> Never dreamed, though right were worsted, wrong
>   would triumph[1],
> Held we fall to rise, are baffled to fight better,
>   Sleep to wake.

[1] As Hardy remarked: "That was a lucky dreamlessness for Browning". And how *can* one march except "breast forward"?

BROWNING

And so with a final flourish that hot-hearted little gentleman strides out into the ironic silence of Eternity; leaving behind him, fortunately, a few human figures that still speak to us, a few lyrics that still sing.

What a creature of contradictions he seems to-day to look back on!—a poet who now sings like an angel, now talks like poor Poll; who could write magnificent dramatic monologues, and yet dramas (like *A Blot in the 'Scutcheon*) that maunder beyond belief; whose psychology is at once so subtle and so superficial; who bared his soul to the world in a hundred transparent disguises and yet denounced, with a peck at Shakespeare, the mere notion that he could unlock his heart; who garbed himself in eccentricity, and yet fled at first sight from the coasts of Bohemia. One doubts at times his claim to be called a poet at all. Why did he not write in prose?

Blown harshly keeps the trump its golden cry?
  Tastes sweet the water with such specks of earth?

Often, alas, it does not; but we can separate good from bad. Indeed we must. And, after all, to the author of things like *The Lost Mistress, Love among the Ruins, A Toccata of Galuppi's, Porphyria's Lover, Childe Roland,* and *St Martin's Summer,* much may be forgiven, even his complete works. For his poetry seems to me

37

like the dry bed of an Alpine torrent down which a flood of vast, untamed energy has roared and foamed itself away, leaving a desolation of dead and bleaching stones; yet with here and there a narrow channel where a rush of waters still spins and dances, bright and living, towards its eternal goal.

III

ARNOLD

Je ne puis approuver que ceux qui cherchent en gémissant.

PASCAL.

"Your Middle-Class man thinks it the highest pitch of development of civilization when his letters are carried twelve times a day from Islington to Camberwell and from Camberwell to Islington, and if railway trains run to and fro between them every quarter of an hour. He thinks it is nothing that the trains only carry him from an illiberal, dismal life at Islington to an illiberal, dismal life at Camberwell." Here rings out a new note of rebellion amid the complacent peace of the Victorians. The man who wrote that had not been, like Browning, a happy little boy in this same Camberwell, already gratifying his taste for the grotesque by keeping queer pets, and preserved by the most indulgent of parents from the rigours of a public school; nor again, like Tennyson, a gloomy little boy growing up in a Lincolnshire rectory under a father so melancholy that the child would lie sometimes on the graves in Somersby Churchyard, sobbing to be dead; Matthew Arnold was very differently educated in the monastic culture of Rugby under his father the great Doctor, the editor of Thucydides and the author of six volumes of sermons. That boyhood stamped him for life. To the end, like his father, he kept this mixture of literature and dogma; to the end, like Milton, he remained half Greek and half Hebrew, half poet and half prophet. This Biblical element in Arnold made him, like Tennyson and Browning, too prone to preach: but he remains a contrast to them in other ways. He was more cultivated, both by nature and by nurture. His manner was exquisite; maddening, some thought. "Damn this fop!" cried his opponents in controversy, "can nobody annoy him?" George Sand likened him in youth to "a young Milton on his travels". "I should not dare", said Crabb Robinson, "to be intimate with so clever a young man." And at the close of one of his Oxford lectures, the Master of Jesus was heard murmuring: "The angel ended". In consequence Arnold never shrieks like Tennyson in parts of *Maud*, nor bellows like Browning in *Pacchiarotto*. He had also a clearer mind, more intellectual honesty, more sense of practical reality— as we might expect in a poet whose more active temper turned him also into a critic, a religious controversialist, and an inspector of Nonconformist schools from Yarmouth to Pembroke and from Yorkshire to the Thames, having his children born in lodging-houses and living himself on buns hastily eaten in class-rooms before astonished school-children. "Not here, O Apollo, were haunts meet for thee."

And so, though Arnold remains in many ways a

typical Victorian, a poet struggling with a preacher, he is, I think, less tiresome in his pulpit than Tennyson or Browning. If his greater fastidiousness, his stronger sense of truth, his practical activities prevented him from writing so much poetry, they prevented him also from writing so much bad poetry. And there is a further important difference: Arnold is poignantly conscious of the conflict in himself. It tears him, and he sees it, and it becomes in our eyes all the more painful, but also the more moving—not a muddle, but a battle; not stupid, but tragic. For Arnold was indeed at war with himself; the artist in him with the moralist, the Greek poet with the Hebrew prophet, the lover of Byron and passion and the beauty of the South with the disciple of Wordsworth and knowledge and the sternness of the North. For some, Arnold is a pedant and a prig: really, he was something much more human and more unhappy. It was no saint of marble, nor yet of plaster, who wrote *The New Sirens*, and heard so clearly the music, the passion, the persuasion in their voices as they called to him, "with blown tresses and with beckoning hands"—

> "Come", you say, "opinion trembles,
> Judgement shifts, convictions go:
> Life dries up, the heart dissembles:
> Only what we feel, we know.

> Hath your wisdom known emotions?
> Will it weep our burning tears?
> Hath it drunk of our love-potions
> Crowning moments with the weight of years?"

He makes, in answer, his refusal; but it is not made
without a pang—

> Yes—I muse—and if the dawning
> Into daylight never grew—
> If the glistering wings of morning
> On the dry noon shook their dew—
> If the fits of joy were longer—
> Or the day were sooner done—
> Or, perhaps, if Hope were stronger—
> No weak nursling of an earthly sun...
> Pluck, pluck, cypress, O pale maidens,
> Dusk the hall with yew.

Nor was this conflict in Arnold a mere storm in an
ink-pot, an agony in an armchair: it was fought out
also in Arnold's real life. We know no details. He
wished that no biographer should ever disturb his
dust; he wished in vain, of course; but the evidence
remains often scanty. He has, however, traced for us
himself, in that series of lyrics called *Switzerland*, the
shadowy outline of the struggle between his love for a
French girl he met there, Marguerite, and his sense
that her past with others made impossible a future
for him and her together. Here too in the end he
tears himself free—

ARNOLD

Me let no half-effac'd memories cumber!
  Fled, fled at once, be all vestige of thee—
Deep be the darkness, and still be the slumber—
  Dead be the past and its phantoms to me!

Then, when we meet, and thy look strays towards me,
  Scanning my face and the changes wrought there—
Who, let me say, *is this Stranger regards me,*
  With the grey eyes, and the lovely brown hair?

Just as his own Margaret in *The Forsaken Merman*
breaks away from the unconsecrated love that she
leaves lonely for ever beneath the waves, so between
Marguerite and himself Arnold set "the unplumb'd,
salt, estranging sea". He loved again; he married;
and, to make marriage possible, he gave himself up
to sit in class-rooms while Nonconformist School-
masters lectured before him on indiarubber and
the Gunpowder Plot. He had conquered; but he
remembered.

Calm's not life's crown, though calm is well.

He still heard out of the distance of the past that
voice loved once so well—

Say, has some wet bird-haunted English lawn
Lent it the music of its birds at dawn?

He told himself tales of long-parted lovers joined
again in the sunset of their days, of Iseult tossing
through the surf of the Atlantic once more to
Tristram's arms. He felt desperately the loneliness

45

of all human life, the need for some hand to touch in the darkness of its desolation, whether Marguerite's or another's—

Ah, love, let us be true
To one another! For the world which seems
To lie before us like a land of dreams,
So various, so beautiful, so new,
Hath really neither joy, nor love, nor light,
Nor certitude, nor peace, nor help for pain;
And we are here as on a darkling plain
Swept with confused alarms of struggle and flight,
Where ignorant armies clash by night.

But to that supreme cry of Arnold's loneliness, the Stoic in him made answer, that the battle in the darkness must none the less be fought on to its lonely end.

We cannot kindle when we will
The fire that in the heart resides;
The spirit bloweth and is still,
In mystery our soul abides:
But tasks in hours of insight will'd
Can be through hours of gloom fulfill'd.

Loneliness, indeed, is not only the doom of man, it is the price of man's greatness—

Alone the sun arises, and alone
Spring the great streams.

And after the battle—what victory, what reward, here and beyond? None, is Arnold's answer—unless it be a little calm, perhaps, before the dreamless calm of all eternity.

> Charge once more, and then be dumb!
> Let the victors when they come,
> When the forts of folly fall,
> Find thy body by the wall.

There is surely something more spirited here than Tennyson's vague gropings for "the larger hope"; something less self-important than Browning's greeting the unseen with a cheer, which seems to me too like putting a paper-hat on the Sphinx.

Arnold may have been a little too sure which, exactly, the Forts of Folly were. That clash of ignorant armies in the gloom was surely a truer, as well as a finer, image of human life with all its blind perplexities. But it is impossible not to respect the man's sincerity. *In Memoriam* is often more beautiful; but beside it the poetry of Arnold, at its best, seems to rise like a mountain-peak, cold and clear in the grey peace of evening, above the musical but bewildered murmurings of a twilit forest. Indeed, as a summary of the essential things in Arnold, I often remember Stevenson's lines on the Highlands of Galloway—

Hills of the sheep, and homes of the ancient, vanished races,
And winds austere and pure.

There the "hills of the sheep" may stand for the influence on Arnold of Wordsworth and the poetry of Westmorland; the "homes of the ancient, vanished races" for that other influence of Greece and Palestine; and the "winds austere and pure" for the breath of Arnold's own spirit.

But although this long struggle in Arnold makes him a more moving figure, the final victory of the Stoic side of him makes him also a little bleak. A larger, healthier nature would, one feels, have reconciled this inner conflict; the victory of ascetic self-discipline involves a defeat of other elements in human nature just as important. Renan says somewhere of Arnold's master, Marcus Aurelius, that he lacked one vital thing—the kiss of a fairy at his birth. Arnold had not been left unkissed; but, no doubt with the able assistance of his father the Headmaster of Rugby, he studied only too successfully at times to forget it. He feels that the world of Nature seems "to bear rather than rejoice"; and we feel the same of him. He does lack gaiety, lightness of touch, the ironic acceptance of a world past our mending, the smile of Montaigne, the laugh of Voltaire, the "feather-pate of folly" that bears the falling sky. It is not really sensible to be always so sadly wise. In real life, indeed, Arnold could smile very charmingly, even at his own expense; "my wife", he would say, "has all my graces and none of my airs"; and he was delighted when on his American tour he found himself compared by a Chicago newspaper to "an elderly macaw pecking at a trellis of grapes". But as a poet, I think, he suffered from this over-austere philosophy of his. It is not, indeed, its sadness that matters. The greatest poetry in the world is largely the saddest; and *The Times* has seldom surpassed its comment on Arnold's *Empedocles*—"He is disgusted with the world; a state of mind with which we have no sympathy whatever". But Arnold's puritanism did damage his verse by giving it a strain of dispirited monotony, just as it certainly warped his criticism. When we listen to him denouncing the letters of Keats, and the circle of Shelley, and the character of Burns, and the lack of character in Coleridge, and the seduction-theme of *Faust*, and the "disrespectability" of Heine, and the "hunger, rebellion, and rage" of poor Charlotte Brontë, we realize with a gasp what a Victorian this satirist of Victorianism could be, what a Philistine this scourge of the Philistines himself always remained. There was justice as well as wit in Swinburne's jest about "David the son of Goliath"; and Chaucer, whom Arnold blamed as having too little "high seriousness", might easily have answered with a smile that his critic had too much. Arnold recognized two main elements in poetry—natural magic and moral profundity; but with his fetish about poetry being "criticism of life" he too often in practice sacrificed the magic to the morals.

This asceticism shows itself even in his style; even here he tended to prefer sackcloth to satin. Sometimes he attained a very happy mean between the two; *Sohrab and Rustum* is a fine thing in this simple grandeur of its style as in other ways; and that great cry of the fallen Sohrab might well be Arnold's own—

> Truth sits upon the lips of dying men,
> And falsehood, while I lived, was far from mine.

But too often his bareness becomes threadbare, and his contempt for the graces too like that of an early Christian hermit sitting in a cell with no furniture but a platter and a pipkin. How could he write things like these?—

> Agamemnon's unhappy,
> Matricidal, world-fam'd,
> Seven-cubit-statur'd son;

or again—

> Sculptors like Phidias,
> Raphaels in shoals,
> Poets like Shakespeare—
> Beautiful souls.

Whole pieces like *Balder* and *Merope* wear the same gaunt, white-washed, work-house air. And yet there are also moments when Arnold grows suddenly rich, and turns from building in corrugated iron, to marble and porphyry. In *The Scholar Gipsy* and *Thyrsis*, those

two laments for a dead age and a dead friend, he
allows himself a new magnificence, of language and
metre alike; rather as some stern St Benedict might
grant to death what he refused to life and permit a
splendour of gold and velvet to glitter on a brother's
funeral-rites. Then Arnold at last becomes as lovely
as sincere, and the disenchantment of old age itself
vanishes before the spell of perfect words.

> Yes, thou art gone! And round me too the night
>   In ever-nearing circle weaves her shade.
>   I see her veil draw soft across the day,
>   I feel her slowly chilling breath invade
>   The cheek grown thin, the brown hair sprent
>   with grey;
>   I feel her finger light
>   Laid pausefully upon life's headlong train;
>   The foot less prompt to meet the morning dew,
>   The heart less bounding at emotion new,
> And hope, once crushed, less quick to spring again.

There, in that lament for the lost Thyrsis, Arnold, it
seems to me, truly and finally found himself. At
last he was content, following Keats, to be, for
moments at least, simply beautiful. To-day his religious discussions are dead. We smile wonderingly at
his attempt to convert the Church of England from
a personal God to "a stream of things not ourselves,
a stream of Tendency making for Righteousness"—
it remains so clear that such a stream, whether or no

it made for Righteousness, was not made for worship.
His criticism, again, is still respected; but it dates.
It is by his poetry that Arnold lives to-day; a poetry
often as bare and rugged as a Greek mountain, but
in its gentler moods recalling those quiet English
waters that flow past Laleham Churchyard where he
lies. In the words of Sir William Watson—

> And nigh to where his bones abide,
> The Thames with its unruffled tide
> Seems like his genius typified,
>   Its strength, its grace,
> Its lucid gleam, its sober pride,
>   Its tranquil pace.

A forgotten poet of an earlier age saw likewise in
the Thames the symbol of these same qualities; and
when we remember that Denham stands, with Waller,
at the opening of our neo-classic age, there is a special
fitness in applying to Arnold, our last great neo-
classic, the famous couplet on that river in Denham's
poem, *Cooper's Hill*—

Though deep, yet clear: though gentle, yet not dull:
Strong without rage: without o'erflowing, full.

But, after all, we need not go to other poets for
rivers; Arnold has himself fashioned the noblest
symbol of his own life in that picture, not of the
Thames, but the Oxus, which leads us so magni-

ficently away from the night-hung battlefield where
Rustum mourns for ever above the son he slew—

But the majestic River floated on,
Out of the mist and hum of that low land,
Into the frosty starlight, and there mov'd,
Rejoicing, through the hush'd Chorasmian waste,
Under the solitary moon: he flow'd
Right for the Polar Star, past Orgunjè,
Brimming, and bright, and large: then sands begin
To hem his watery march, and dam his streams,
And split his currents; that for many a league
The shorn and parcell'd Oxus strains along
Through beds of sand and matted rushy isles—
Oxus, forgetting the bright speed he had
In his high mountain cradle in Pamere,
A foil'd circuitous wanderer—till at last
The long'd-for dash of waves is heard, and wide
His luminous home of waters opens, bright
And tranquil, from whose floor the new-bath'd stars
Emerge, and shine upon the Aral Sea.

IV

CLOUGH

A peine si, nous-mêmes, nous savons comment nous travaillons, comment nous viennent nos idées, comment nous les réalisons; si nous le savions trop bien, nous ne pourrions plus travailler du tout.... Il est d'ailleurs extrêmement dangereux de trop réfléchir sur ses actes, sur sa vie; le Gnothi Seauton est peut-être la sottise la plus délétère qui fût jamais proférée.

RÉMY DE GOURMONT.

Arthur Clough was born on New Year's Day, 1819, of a family connected with John Calvin (there is something both appropriate and ironic in that) and with a Hugh Clough, who was a friend of Cowper and a Fellow of King's, in the chapel of which he lies buried. The poet's mother was a devout, clinging woman with an admiration for stoic courage which led her to regale the little Cloughs with stories of martyrdoms, from Leonidas to Latimer. It is not surprising that Arthur, her favourite, grew into a serious child, too prim to take off his shoes and stockings on the beach, and given to choosing for himself, in games of "Swiss Family Robinson", the part of Ernest. From 1829 to 1837 he was at Rugby under Arnold. It is clear that he was overstrained there, both mentally and morally: of the second his own letters are proof enough. He writes, aged seventeen: "I verily believe my whole being is soaked through with the wishing and hoping and striving to do the school good, or rather to keep it up and hinder it from falling in this, I do think, very critical time, so that all my cares and affections and conversations, thoughts, words and deeds, look to that involuntarily". And again, nine months later: "we are all getting on very pleasantly this half-year, and the school looks remarkably harmless, and everybody inclined to do their best and behave well; which is very delicious". From these delights Clough passed in the next year to Oxford; where this severe young scholar might be found plunging in the wintry Cherwell, or working in a fireless room at Balliol, whence the hardiest visitors fled after a few minutes' exposure. Which is precisely what they were meant to do. But fireless as his rooms might be, Clough was, in his own phrase, drawn "like straw up the draught of a chimney" by a conflagration of another sort—the Oxford Movement. For the influence of Arnold was now succeeded in him by the influence of Newman, as Newman's was in its turn to be replaced by Carlyle's. For the present, Clough emerged with his faith bewildered and his career endangered: instead of a first, which all who knew him had taken for granted, he gained only a second; his father failed in business; he himself failed for a fellowship at Balliol. In the next year, however, 1842, he was elected at Oriel and it was open to him to settle down into the placid, backwater-lily existence of a don. Arnold, his first leader, died this year: his second, Newman, passed over in 1845 to Rome. But Clough had now found his own vocation: he had begun to doubt. New winds of the spirit blew him out of his harbour—the boisterous breath of Carlyle, whirling "Hebrew old clothes" like withered leaves before it; and the calmer influence of Emerson. In 1848, year of revolutions, Clough's religious scepticism had reached a point that made his position at Oriel impossible: he resigned tutorship and fellowship. But the world which now awaited from him a solemn religious apologia stating his position, was somewhat disconcerted to be presented instead with a light-hearted pastoral in mocking hexameters, all about a vacation reading-party of undergraduates—*The Bothie of Tober-na-Vuolich*. Oxford read it with headshaking and judged it (of all things!) "indecent and profane","immoral and communistic".

The next year, 1849, found Clough at Rome; not as a convert to the Roman Church, but as a sympathetic, yet half-cynical spectator of that forlorn defence of the Roman Republic by Garibaldi and Mazzini, which is so vividly painted in Trevelyan's prose and in the verse of Clough's own *Amours de Voyage*.

The rest of his life is less significant—an unhappy, lonely period as head of University Hall in London; a brief migration to Cambridge, U.S.A.; seven quiet and contented years of marriage, with a post in the Education Office; then in 1860–1 a breakdown, a hurried flight abroad, and a resting-place for ever in the Protestant cemetery of Florence, where five months before him Elizabeth Barrett Browning had been laid. Clough was no peer of the two English poets who sleep in the sister-cemetery at Rome; but not even "Adonais" had a nobler dirge than the death of "Thyrsis" drew from the son of that Arnold under whom had begun his troubled experience of life.

But Clough, just as he is finer than most of his poetry, is more interesting than most of his life. He had, one may say, two ruling passions—one, for going his own way and thinking his own thoughts; the other, for going, and for thinking, straight. The moral conscientiousness of the model pupil of Arnold is of no great interest: young prigs, never rare, were particularly plentiful then. But the intense intellectual conscientiousness into which it grew is a far rarer quality: it remains one of the central things in the worth of Clough's poetry and in the unhappiness of his life.

It was, indeed, this unresting critical honesty of mind that rescued him from the effects of a system of education about which he later retained no illusions. Seventy years before Lytton Strachey, whom some thought so unfair, Arnold's own pupil criticized no less incisively, through the mouth of the Uncle in *Dipsychus*, Arnold's treatment of schoolboys as miserable little sinners with souls to be saved: "They're all so pious...they seem to me a sort of hobbadi-hoy cherub, too big to be innocent, and too simple for anything else. They're full of the notion of the world being so wicked, and of their taking a higher line as they call it. I only fear they'll never take any line at all. . . . Why didn't he flog them and hold his tongue? Flog them he did, but why preach?" From this Rugbeian elephantiasis of the conscience Clough recovered; but he seems himself to have doubted whether he recovered completely. One cannot be too careful about teasing fiction into autobiography; but the hero of *Dipsychus* is certainly in part a self-portrait:

> He was a sort of moral prig, I've heard,
> Till he was twenty-five: and even then
> He never entered into life as most men.
> That is the reason why he fails so soon.

Similarly, in *Mari Magno*:

> He now, o'ertasked at school, a serious boy,
> A sort of after-boyhood to enjoy
> Appeared. . . .
> With all his eager notions still there went
> A self-correcting and ascetic bent,
> That from the obvious good still led astray,
> And set him travelling on the longest way.

Whatever this may be as poetry, as psychology it rings true enough. How much of Clough's final character came to him from birth, how much from Rugby, only a modern biographer would be rash enough to estimate. Certainly Clough believed in an inherited lack of vitality. "Take care", he writes to his brother, "you never say 'It's too much trouble'— 'I can't be bothered', which are tolerably old favourites of yours, and, indeed, of all who have any Perfect blood in them." (Perfect was his mother's maiden name.) The peculiar misfortune was that one by nature so scrupulous and doubtful should have been thrown by destiny first into the most over-scrupulous of schools, and then into a society hag-ridden by religious doubt. This child of Diffidence was bred up by Too-good, then sent to live in Doubt-ing Castle. Poor relations of Hamlet are tediously numerous; but Clough was no ignoble member of that family. He too lacked, not will, but eyelids—the power to stop looking and shut his eyes and leap. And he too found his malady completed by his own aware-ness of it, by the self-knowledge that he was born

> To finger idly some old Gordian knot,
> Unskilled to sunder and too weak to cleave.

Sceptics should take care to inherit a sanguine temperament. Clough lacked the wise frivolity of Lucian or Montaigne or Voltaire—"I do not greatly think about Montaigne". Nature had denied to that earnest soul the animal spirits that enable happier men to be as foolish as a foolish world requires. In the words of *Thyrsis*:

CLOUGH

Some life of men unblest
He knew, which made him droop and filled his head.
He went: his piping took a troubled sound
Of storms that rage outside our happy ground;
He could not wait their passing, he is dead.

It was not only religious uncertainty that tormented him. Even in love, where few men find any difficulty in being foolish enough, his intellectual conscience pursues him with doubts whether his passion is not (characteristic word) "factitious". The real Clough did in the end get happily married (how much by his own doing we cannot know); but the hero of *Amours de Voyage,* one of his many self-portraits, ends more deeply lost than ever in the doubt that stands inscribed on its title-page—"Il doutait de tout, même de l'amour". The "factitious" pursues him as the Furies Orestes. Love, to meet his demands, has to be far too true ever to run smooth:

I tremble for something factitious,
Some malpractice of heart, some illegitimate process.
We are so prone to these things with our terrible
notions of duty.

He certainly feels something: but what is it?

Well, I know after all it is only juxtaposition.
Juxtaposition in short: and what is juxtaposition?

What, indeed? He might have found an answer in a

poetess he knew, the first of poetesses, in that quivering poem which begins:

> God is not more blessèd than is the lover
> Sitting, looking into thy face before him.

But it would have been no use. The unhappy ending of *Amours de Voyage* is a foregone conclusion:

After all perhaps there was something factitious about
    it;
I have had pain, it is true: I have wept, and so have
    the actors.

As with love, so with politics. Clough is that "Republican Friend" to whom Arnold addressed his sonnets of 1848. But in the republican Rome of 1849 Clough was not one of the heroic geese who might perhaps save the Capitol. He sympathized; he understood; indeed, he understood far too well.

Victory! Victory! Victory!—Ah, but it is, believe me,
Easier, easier far, to intone the chant of the martyr
Than to indite any paean of any victory. Death may
Sometimes be nobler; but life, at the best, will appear
    an illusion. . . .
    The smoke of the sacrifice rises to heaven
Of a sweet savour, no doubt, to Somebody, but on
    the altar,
Lo, there is nothing remaining but ashes and dirt and
    ill odour.

Some of us may, perhaps, find that odour not unfamiliar, remembering 1919 and 1946; and, after

64

seeing Mussolini follow Mazzini, may wonder if
Clough was, after all, so wrong as our fathers must
have thought.

Whither depart the souls of the brave that die in the
    battle,
Die in the lost, lost fight for the cause that perishes
    with them;
Are they upborne from the field on the slumberous
    pinions of angels
Unto a far-off home where the weary rest from their
    labour,
And the deep wounds are healed, and the bitter and
    burning moisture
Wiped from the generous eyes? Or do they linger,
    unhappy,
Pining and haunting the grave of their bygone hope
    and endeavour?
  All declamation, alas. . . . !
Whither depart the brave?—God knows; I certainly
    do not.

"He that looks too long into the abyss", said
Nietzsche, "in the end the abyss shall look into him."
But that, through life, was the one thing Clough never
hesitated to do, long and steadily, come what might.
Honesty, coupled with a sense of humour which first
appears in his mature writing, like a sun first seen at
noon on a grey day, is what ennobled the vision of
life which he expressed so often in verse and sometimes in poetry. Like Samuel Butler, he too pursued

"the understanding that surpasses any peace"; like
Bishop Butler, he also passionately felt—"Things and
actions are what they are and the consequences of
them will be what they will be: why then should we
desire to be deceived?" In his own homely phrase:

> But play no tricks upon thy soul, O man,
> Let fact be fact, and life the thing it can.

Or again, in one of his finer flashes:

> It fortifies my soul to know
> That, though I perish, truth is so.

Or yet once more, in a typical letter: "I think I must
have been getting into a little mysticism lately. It
won't do: twice two are four, all the world over, and
there's no harm in its being so; 'tisn't the devil's doing
that it is; *il faut s'y soumettre*, and all right". No wonder
he loved the eighteenth century and thought it a good
training for a poet to copy out some Goldsmith every
day; no wonder pupils of his remembered how at
some wild opinion in their essays he would only say
in his quiet searching way: "Ah then, you think so?"

The result of too much good sense is disillusion: the
sugar for disillusion is irony. It is a bitter sweetening;
but it serves. Eighteenth-century France can illustrate
that. And Clough, though he could never be epi-
cureanly gay, developed a pleasantly ironic humour;
genial in the *Bothie*, more flippantly bitter in *Amours
de Voyage*, bitterer still in *Dipsychus*, but most pointed

66

of all perhaps in *The Latest Decalogue,* with that admirable climax of sneering feminine rhymes:

> Thou shalt not covet: but tradition
> Approves all forms of competition.

But Clough can never play Mephistopheles for long; there is too much of the tenderer Margaret in him, too much of that wistfulness which finds its utterance in the three poems of his that all the world still knows —*Peschiera, Qua Cursum Ventus,* and *Say not the struggle naught availeth.*

It is, then, as a human document rather than as literature that much of Clough's work can be enjoyed to-day—as the utterance of a mind preserved from softness by its wit, from ineffectiveness by its courage and good sense. Technically, Clough's verse can at times be atrocious—

> Had miscellaneous experience had
> Of human acts, good half, and half of bad.

But he is sometimes lovely, seldom dull, never false. Thus *The Bothie of Tober-na-Vuolich,* if read, as it should be read, for nothing more serious than amusement, has a way of startling one every now and then with glimpses of sudden beauty, or with sudden depths—

> Perfect as picture, as vision entrancing that comes to
> the sightless
> Through the great granite jambs, the stream, the
> glen, and the mountain.

The next instant, like his mountain-stream, his hurrying hexameters will tumble laughing down bathos after bathos; until they foam out again into some momentary loveliness, or run more deeply and slowly through a stretch of quiet reflection. For even here in the wilderness, though less harshly, echo the cryings of Carlyle and the questionings of 1848: even here is debated that eternal problem of the price of civilization in terms of human misery. The Socialistic young hero, destined to marry a Highland lass in the end, is temporarily bewitched by a girl of the upper class.

Often I find myself saying and know not myself as I
    say it,
What of the poor and the weary? Their labour and
    pain is needed.
Perish the poor and the weary! What can they better
    than perish?
Perish in labour for her, who is worth the destruction
    of empires?
What! for a mite, for a mote, an impalpable odour of
    honour,
Armies shall bleed; cities burn; and the soldier red
    from the storming
Carry hot rancour and lust into chambers of mothers
    and daughters. . . .
Yea—and shall hodmen in beer-shops complain of a
    glory denied them,
Which could not ever be theirs more than now it is
    theirs as spectators?

Which could not be in all earth, if it were not for
    labour of hodmen?
And I find myself saying, and what I am saying dis-
    cern not,
Dig in thy deep dark prison, O miner! and finding be
    thankful;
Though unpolished by thee, by thee unseen in per-
    fection,
While thou art eating black bread in the poisonous
    air of thy cavern,
Far away glitters the gem on the peerless neck of a
    Princess.
Dig, and starve, and be thankful; it is so and thou
    hast been aiding.

That problem, surely, has still a familiar ring to-day.

Clough put a good deal into this poem; for, indeed, it contained a good deal of himself. He had
taken a reading-party to Glen Urquhart the year
before; several of the characters are portraits; even
the hero's romance with a Highland girl recalls the
lyric ὁ Θεὸς μετὰ σοῦ in a way which suggests that a
real experience lay behind. But I suppose *The Bothie*
finds few readers to-day: and *Amours de Voyage* even
fewer, though it seems to me better still. The idea of
a novel in hexameter letters hardly stirs the blood;
yet I feel Clough's hexameters to be the only successful specimens of their kind in English. For
English hexameters cannot be taken seriously. That
is exactly why they suit so well the half-mocking tone

of these two poems; and just because their tone is so largely burlesque, when it does at moments become serious, the contrast is strong enough to make us for a moment take them seriously too. This contrast runs all through the action of *Amours de Voyage*—the abortive, very English love affair of this "too quick despairer", seen against the background of the vain heroism of the brief Roman Republic. It is a slight, amusingly told story, made to serve as a thread for Clough's reflections on life, which form the real heart of the poem up to its stoical conclusion:

Shall we come out of it all, some day, as one does
    from a tunnel?
Will it be all at once, without our doing or asking,
We shall behold clear day, the trees and meadows
    about us,
And the faces of friends, and the eyes we loved look-
    ing at us?
Who knows? Who can say? It will not do to suppose
    it. . . .

  Not as the Scripture says, is, I think, the fact. Ere
    our death-day,
Faith, I think, does pass, and Love, but Knowledge
    abideth,
Let us seek Knowledge;—the rest may come and go
    as it happens,
Knowledge is hard to seek, and harder yet to adhere to.
Knowledge is painful often; and yet when we know
    we are happy.

Seek it, and leave mere Faith and Love to come with
    the chances.
As for Hope—to-morrow I hope to be starting for
    Naples.

So too, under the Roman Empire, Virgil, it is said,
likewise concluded, "All things grow a weariness,
except to understand"—"omnia lassant praeter in-
tellegere": so too, under the Third Republic, Proust
likewise turned away from the world—to understand.
Is it really the wisest course? That is another question. But I have an affection for *Amours de Voyage*. It
is not the sort of work to appeal to either the popin-
jays or the pedants in modern criticism. It is too
human. So much the better. One may like a poet to
wear other than daisy-chains, even though at times
he clanks and stumbles in them. Pure Beauty left too
long alone is always liable to be found fondling hairy
ears, in a union of null perfection and perfect nullity.

    The two other long poems published after Clough's
death are both unfinished and both inferior. *Dipsychus*,
"the Doubled-souled", an adaptation of the idea of
Faust, with a characteristic twist leaves it in doubt
whether its Mephistopheles is really a devil, or simply
the Spirit of Good Sense. But though there are
moments when here too Clough's irony rings home,
as in the passage where Mephistopheles insists that
the hero shall take holy orders, the poem as a whole

goes too much in dressing-gown and slippers. Similarly, *Mari Magno*, with its remote mixture of Chaucer and Crabbe, is to-day but a barren ocean to plough: yet there remain fine things, now widely forgotten, in the shorter poems—among them that fragment *The Shadow*, whose opening dignity Clough never equalled again:

> I dreamed a dream: I dreamt that I espied,
> Upon a stone that was not rolled aside,
> A Shadow sit upon a grave—a Shade
> As thin, as unsubstantial, as of old
> Came, the Greek poet told,
> To lick the life-blood in the trench Ulysses made—

Then once more the serious features relax into the old ironic smile, the agonized flippancy of Hamlet; for the shade of the risen Jesus cannot explain Himself; the priests alone show no tremor of doubt in themselves or of belief in Him—

> As for the Shade, who trusted such narration?
> Except, of course, in ancient revelation.

To-day, as we look back, Clough seems the poet of a promise unfulfilled—of a promise cut short, not like that of Keats by death, but by lack of vitality. His later work steadily weakens; and there is little reason to suppose that longer life would have meant for him longer memory. At times he seems made to fit his friend's phrase of Shelley—"an ineffectual angel"—

and yet Clough was of sturdier stuff than that implies. His was less the faint heart that wins no fair lady, than the eternal doubt which lady was indeed fair. It was no mere "angel" that impressed the critical Matthew Arnold with the sense that there had never been "purer or more subtle soul", and left his mark even on the rough granite of Carlyle's mind. For us he remains the impersonation of an age when religious doubt was not, as now, a rare and mild green-sickness, but a crippling, even a fatal malady. We are not cleverer; we are harder, disillusioned, indifferent. The age of crusades is over: few lament it. But a crusade was what Clough longed for:

> We ask action
> And dream of arms and conflict; and string up
> All self-devotion's muscles; and are set
> To fold up papers.

The Crimean War came: but it set Clough to string up, not "self-devotion's muscles", but (as Mr Strachey's readers will remember) the brown-paper parcels of Miss Florence Nightingale. Perhaps the truth is that he took life too seriously, and art not seriously enough. The air of the amateur clings about him: he could not, like happier artists, forget the whole round globe in carving some cherry-stone. He seems at times a half-hewn Matthew Arnold, left lying in the quarry. He *is* Hamlet, Hamlet with a touch of Polonius—not Shakespeare. His sadness grows monotonous. "Laugh, my young friends", says Nietzsche again, "if you are at all determined to remain pessimists."

Laughter indeed is easy for the insensitive, the world provides no lack of subjects.

> But men at whiles are sober
>   And think by fits and starts;
> And, when they think, they fasten
>   Their hands upon their hearts.

V

COVENTRY PATMORE

Maudit soit à jamais le rêveur inutile
Qui voulut le premier, dans sa stupidité,
S'éprenant d'un problème insoluble et stérile,
Aux choses de l'amour mêler l'honnêteté!

BAUDELAIRE

Coventry Patmore was born in 1823. His father was a writer of a sort, described by Thackeray as "that murderer". But Mr Patmore senior was not really a murderer, merely the blundering second of Lockhart's friend Christie in his duel with Scott, editor of the *London Magazine*. Scott was killed and it was thought, with some reason, that Patmore might have prevented things from going so far.

The first recorded words of his small son were "Coventry is a clever fellow". That was an opinion Patmore never changed: and indeed, if one could believe his autobiographical stories, it was early deserved. By fifteen, he says, he had read all English literature and discovered a new chloride of bromine. He also became a youthful agnostic until, opening a devotional book one day, it struck him what an exceedingly fine thing it would be if there were a God. That was enough. There must be.

He went to school in France; and became anti-French. The first angel in his life appeared early—a certain Miss Gore.

> At nine years old I was love's willing page,
> For poets love earlier than other men.

In 1844, aged twenty-one, he published his first book of poems. They were cursed by *Blackwood's* in best *Blackwood's* style: "This is the life which the slime of the Keateses and Shelleys of former times

77

has fecundated. The result was predicted a quarter of a century ago in this magazine—nothing is so tenacious of life as the spawn of frogs."

A year later, in 1845, his father was ruined and fled abroad, leaving Coventry to shift for himself. The young man was reduced at one point to three and sixpence in the world. With characteristic bravado he spent it on ices. He made friends in London with the melancholy Tennyson; and he made a more useful friendship with Mrs Procter. "Who is your lean young friend with the frayed wrist-cuffs?" asked Monckton Milnes of her one day. The result of her kindly advocacy was a post for Patmore in the printed-books department of the British Museum.

This enabled him in 1847 to marry his "Angel in the House", a Miss Emily Andrews, daughter of the Dissenting minister who taught Ruskin Greek. She was herself to become the author of a *Servants' Behaviour Book*, of verses for children by "Mrs Motherly", and of moral stories; of one, for instance, about a race of men supplied with tails which, by registering their emotions, made hypocrisy impossible. Coventry tested her fitness by lending her Emerson's *Essays*: she passed triumphantly, choosing the same passages to approve or disapprove as he.

In 1853 he published *Tamerton Church Tower*. In the next year he began to print his famous *Angel in the House*. The reviewers did not greatly take to the

Angel: but the public simply adored her and by 1896 had bought over 250,000 copies.

Meanwhile, in 1862, the real Angel, the first Mrs Patmore, died; saying with shrewd and generous foresight—"I leave my wedding-ring to your second wife with my love and blessing".

At the same time she was saddened by another prevision no less shrewd. Aubrey de Vere and Manning had been trying to convert Patmore to Rome: Mrs Patmore, true daughter of Dissent, had boldly met their arguments. But now on her death-bed, "When I am gone", she said sadly, "they will get you; and I shall see you no more."

They did. Although, rather thanklessly, Patmore afterwards maintained that his conversion had only been retarded, not hastened, by these efforts of Manning and Aubrey de Vere.

Three years later he met in Rome a certain Miss Byles, who at one time, before Manning himself went over, had some prospects of becoming the second Mrs Manning. In her Patmore discerned "a Catholic beauty"—as indeed he did in most things he liked— even in things as unlikely, one would have thought, to be "Catholic" as the Aphrodite of Melos. But to his horror he found that, instead of being the companion of a rich lady, she was rich herself. He fled; and it needed all the efforts of his friends to bring the errant lover back to the altar, where the ceremony

79

was performed by Manning himself. Patmore was now able to leave the British Museum and settle as a country gentleman in Ashdown Forest.

In 1873, deciding that *The Angel in the House* was not orthodox, he made a bonfire of all copies within reach. But there is not much point in burning a book with a circulation of a quarter of a million. The *Angel* would have survived the furnace of Nebuchadnezzar.

However in 1877 Patmore produced a new volume of verse so utterly different that no one would have guessed its authorship—*The Unknown Eros*.

Then, in 1880 the second Mrs Patmore died; though not before Coventry Patmore had fallen in love with the third, a friend of his daughter's, whom he married in the following year. "Why, papa", said Piffie, his small son by this last wife, "you're half as bad as Henry VIII."

In 1887–8 he burnt his mystical prose work *Sponsa Dei, The Bride of God*, on his favourite theme of the analogy between the soul's relation to God and the wife's relation to her husband; partly because of the comment passed on it by Gerard Manley Hopkins—"That's telling secrets."

At seventy, vigorous as ever, the poet seems to have fallen in love with Alice Meynell. Three years later, in 1896, he died and was buried in the robe of a Franciscan.

COVENTRY PATMORE

It has been said that Coventry Patmore was a queer combination of Turkish Pasha and Anglican clergyman. "Anglican clergyman", however, I feel to be hardly right. Perhaps one might better say a combination of Catholic mystic and Colonel Blimp.

For his views on mundane things were fantastically violent and reactionary. "The whole population of England", he observes, "now seems to be chronically drunk every Saturday, Sunday, and Monday, Feast-day and Fast. It is very lucky." Similarly in his eyes Disraeli's Reform Bill was a step towards the final ruin of English liberties. It even wrung from him an ode called "1867", with the spirited opening—

> In the year of the great crime
> When the false English Nobles and their Jew,
> By God demented, slew
> The trust they stood twice pledged to keep from
> wrong.

Yet if Disraeli was bad, Gladstone was no better. One of the first sentences taught to Patmore's Benjamin, little Piffie, was "Damn Gladstone and Home Rule!"

Educated women, again, were as bad as working-class voters—"There are few more damnable heresies than the doctrine of the equality of man and woman." "If there is anything God hates utterly, it is a clever woman." (This however he later retracted.)

Even children were little better—"I have indeed

very little respect for children. Their so-called inno-
cence is want of practice rather than inclination, and
all bad passions seem to me to be more violent in
children than in men and women, and more wicked
because in more immediate conjunction with the
divine vision." A curious way of looking both forward
to the discoveries of Freud and back to the savageries
of St Augustine.

Not even animals escaped. Patmore railed and
raged against the S.P.C.A.—"After hearing of one
of their more flagrant acts of mercy", he would say,
"I go down to the stableyard and thrash the dogs
all round." At this point, however, caution becomes
necessary. Clearly he said such things largely to make
the flesh of visitors creep.

All the same, his list of anathemas included even
the priests of his new faith. "All Poets and Prophets
have hated priests." Accordingly he paradoxically
approved Gibbon. And when a fire burnt some
church property, he observed with ferocious humour
that the priests had done it, for the insurance money.

In fact he was as fierce and "humorous" as any
character in Ben Jonson.

Even his appetites are Blimpish. He complains
furiously of the food at Nice. "At the hour I require
a pound of steak and a pint of ale, I go into the most
likely-looking shop and, after walking three times
round a table on which are thirty or forty different

plates, I select what looks the most substantial—and bite a brown bladder of air." No wonder he talks lovingly elsewhere of "the roast beef of Shakespeare".

He could, however, be "humorous" in the modern as well as the Elizabethan sense: and when the French Ultramontane paper, *L'Univers*, once solemnly devoted two columns to a "beautiful English Catholic tradition" of how the dormouse got a furry tail, the tradition in question turned out to be merely a piece of Patmore's fun. The dormouse, he had related, was so horrified at the sight of Eve reaching for the Apple that it hid its eyes with its tail: and was in that instant miraculously given a furry one to form a better screen.

And yet this humorous beef-eater remained also a mystic, with sensitive, finely chiselled features, who sought his obsession, "the Nuptial Idea", alike in Heaven and on earth as pertinaciously as Sir Thomas Browne hunted quincunxes in every corner of the Universe, from constellations to nut-crackers.

To Patmore, his first love was a preparation for his wife; and his relation to his wife was in its turn a preparation for his relation to God. For God feels towards each human soul as lover feels towards mistress. Thus the Divine election corresponds to the lover's desire. In either case all sins in the beloved can be forgiven, except only infidelity (how much philosophy is built on pretending quite different senses of the same word are the same!); and in either case the lover desires the sight rather than the service of the beloved—Mary rather than Martha. In both relationships the lover commands, while the beloved persuades (at least in the Patmore household). Again love, both human and divine, holds symbols especially dear. And finally it sees best in the dark.

And so forth. I suppose modern psychology might diagnose these as the fantasies of a repressed homosexual. But Patmore was no great lover of reasoning. "The devil", he said, "is the only being purely reasonable and analytic, and therefore *is* the devil."

As might be expected, Patmore's poetry shows the same strange combination of tempest and tea-cup, of Himalaya and suburb.

Tamerton Church Tower, indeed, is not important: though the reader interested in character smiles a little ironically over this story of a man who rides across Exmoor, marries, loses his wife in a boating-trip, and rides sadly home again with the vision of his next wife already hovering on the horizon. In Patmore's imagination, as in his life, casualties were quickly replaced, with a determination that would certainly have won the admiring sympathy of the Wife of Bath.

Next comes that great epic of uxoriousness, *The Angel in the House*.

The very idea of it thrilled Patmore. Here was

the finest subject in the world, left unclaimed by
thirty centuries of poets, for him, Coventry Patmore,
to pick up. He felt like the ghost of Odysseus in
Plato's "Vision of Er"; who, when he came, last of
all, to choose a career for his next incarnation, found
flung aside by those before him the very one that he
most coveted—the life of an ordinary man. For
Patmore's supreme subject was none other than re-
spectably married love, or love that leads to marriage.

> "Learn that to me, though born so late,
>   There does, beyond desert, befall
> (May my great fortune make me great!)
>   The first of themes, sung last of all.
> In green and undiscover'd ground,
>   Yet near where many others sing,
> I have the very well-head found
>   Whence gushes the Pierian Spring."
> Then she: "What is it, Dear? The Life
>   Of Arthur, or Jerusalem's Fall?"
> "Neither: your gentle self, my Wife,
>   And love, that grows from one to all."

It was a happy belief for Patmore. It enabled him
to write with pleasure—one of the pleasantest things
in life; and to be read with pleasure by a quarter
of a million purchasers—which may have been even
pleasanter.

But it was not a very happy belief for his poetry.

The first part of the poem tells the love, as uneventfully smooth as its hymn-metre octosyllabics, of a

comfortable young gentleman, with six hundred a year and a prospective seat in Parliament, for one of the three daughters of a Dean: whom he duly weds without meeting any obstacles beyond a cynical aunt, a penniless naval cousin for rival, his own shyness, and the lady's very proper coyness. If the poem had a coat-of-arms, it might well be a piece of bread-and-butter rampant.

The hero's character is very like the author's.

> I laugh'd and sigh'd; for I confess
>   I never went to Ball, or Fête,
> Or Show, but in pursuit express
>   Of my predestinated mate;
> And thus to me, who had in sight
>   The happy chance upon the cards,
> Each beauty blossom'd in the light
>   Of tender personal regards;
> And, in the records of my breast,
>   Red-letter'd, eminently fair,
> Stood sixteen, who, beyond the rest,
>   By turns till then had been my care:
> At Berlin three, one at St Cloud,
>   At Chatteris, near Cambridge, one,
> At Ely four, in London two,
>   Two at Bowness, in Paris none.

There follow abysses of bathos, such as—

> Our witnesses the Cook and Groom,
>   We sign'd the lease for seven years more;

or

And words were growing vain, when Briggs,
    Factotum, Footman, Butler, Groom,
Who press'd the cyder, fed the pigs,
    Preserv'd the rabbits, drove the brougham,
And help'd, at need, to mow the lawns,
    And sweep the paths and thatch the hay,
Here brought the Post down;

or the climax, when the proud husband buys his
Dulcinea a pair of sand-shoes—

I, while the shop-girl fitted on
    The sand-shoes, look'd where, down the bay,
The sea glow'd with a shrouded sun.
    "I'm ready, Felix; will you pay?"
That was my first expense for this
    Sweet Stranger, now my three days' Wife.
How light the touches are that kiss
    The music from the chords of life!

Worst of all, perhaps, are the closing lines of Part I—

But here their converse had its end;
    For, crossing the Cathedral Lawn,
There came an ancient college-friend,
    Who, introduced to Mrs Vaughan,
Lifted his hat, and bow'd and smiled,
    And fill'd her kind large eyes with joy
By patting on the cheek her child,
    With, "Is he yours, this handsome boy?"

Had it all been like this, *The Angel in the House*
would remain merely a curiosity like Tupper's *Pro-verbial Philosophy* or Montgomery's *Omnipresence of the*

Deity. But Patmore interspersed a number of lyrics, like Greek choruses, between his cantos. And some of these show a very different degree of sensitiveness and subtlety.

> Not in the crises of events,
>   Of compass'd hopes, or fears fulfill'd,
> Or acts of gravest consequence,
>   Are life's delight and depth reveal'd.
> The day of days was not the day;
>   That went before, or was postponed;
> The night Death took our lamp away
>   Was not the night on which we groan'd.
> I drew my bride, beneath the moon,
>   Across my threshold; happy hour!
> But, ah, the walk that afternoon
>   We saw the water-flags in flower!

This again, as a versification of mathematics, would have tickled a Metaphysical poet:

> I sigh'd, "Immeasurable bliss
>   Gains nothing by becoming more!
> Millions have meaning; after this
>   Cyphers forget the integer."

This also:

> "I saw you take his kiss!" "'Tis true."
>   "O, modesty!" "'Twas strictly kept:
> He thought me asleep; at least, I knew.
>   He thought I thought he thought I slept."

The second half of the *Angel* makes an even feebler story. It is a novel in letters, infinitely inferior to Clough's *Amours de Voyage*, and tells how the rejected rival of Part I, the naval cousin Frederick, consoles himself with a naval chaplain's daughter given to dropping her "h"s, but after all makes a happy marriage of it. This idyll ends with yet another marriage, between their son and the daughter of the hero and the Angel of Part I. The grand climax is a sermon for his grandchildren's wedding by the Dean.

Such is the poem which Patmore hoped would eclipse Dante's *Divine Comedy*. The cruel might say it was certainly a divine comedy.

Indeed a certain Mr Chorley *was* very cruel in the *Athenaeum*, where he reviewed the *Angel* in verse printed as prose: "The gentle reader we apprize that this new Angel in the House contains a tale not very wise about a Person and a Spouse. The author, gentle as a lamb, has managed his rhymes to fit and haply fancies he has writ another In Memoriam."

Tennyson himself growled that some of its lines seemed hammered up out of old nail heads. Carlyle grunted approval. Rossetti parodied—

> Of love which never finds its published close
> What sequel—and how many?

And Swinburne also parodied in his *Heptalogia* what he called these "Idylls of the Dining Room and the Deanery".

The truth is that Patmore over-estimated what a treasure-trove his subject was. "Happy is the people", says the proverb, "that has no history." Conversely, happy people seldom have much history. And even in Part II, where Patmore allows some unhappiness, the deadly banality persists.

Of two persons threatening marriage Mrs Carlyle remarks somewhere in her letters that they seem contemplating "a lawful catastrophe". To Patmore marriage was the reverse of a catastrophe: but his poem rather lacks one.

Marvell may write—

> My love is of a birth as rare
> As 'tis for object strange and high:
> It was begotten of Despair
> Upon Impossibility.

But that is just what Patmore's love is not.

Swinburne may cry—

> Time turns the old things to derision
> And our loves into corpses or wives,
> And marriage and death and division
> Make barren our lives.

He is being immoral, as Plato says poets nearly always are: but he is at least being a poet, and the lyrical cry is in it.

And when Meredith wrote of his own marriage in *Modern Love*, in a tone the exact opposite of Patmore's, he made a bitter success out of his love's failure, where Patmore makes a sugary failure out of his success.

It is not that wedded love cannot make a good subject. But neither was it really, as Patmore pretended, such a new subject; three thousand years earlier in Homer's Hector and Andromache, or in the Odysseus who leaves Calypso, despite her offer of eternal life, to go back to an ageing Penelope, there are already far finer tributes to human loyalty, without any of Patmore's treacly sentiment. Only Homer saw, what the modern poet failed to see, that intensity needs suffering and that poetry needs dignity.

Perhaps Patmore came in the end to feel that. At all events he left the first grand scheme of his *Angel* incomplete. And when he next writes poetry, he shows a quite new personality; so totally different is *The Unknown Eros*.

For here he passes from hymn-tune simplicity to complicated "Pindaric" metres; from the plainest language to the purple patch; from obvious and parochial themes to cosmic mysteries.

The gain is enormous.

Of course there are links between the two. *The Angel* was concerned to prove that Heaven exists in married love: *The Unknown Eros* is in part concerned to prove that married love exists in Heaven. The New Testament might say what it might: but a

Heaven without marriage would have been to
Coventry Patmore no Heaven at all.

Yet purely as poetry the later volume displays real
eloquence. Patmore has found style. Even the
moments of typical Patmorish tantrums are vivid.
For example he thinks little of astronomy. Indeed he
likes Coleridge's rather cheap notion that the stars
were created simply "to make dirt cheap". But
biology and the microscope seem to him quite another
matter—for these are the science of *Life*!

> Not greatly moved with awe am I
> To learn that we may spy
> Five thousand firmaments beyond our own.
> The best that's known
> Of the heavenly bodies does them credit small.
> View'd close, the Moon's fair ball
> Is of ill objects worst,
> A corpse in Night's highway, naked, fire-scarr'd,
>   accurst;
> And now they tell
> That the Sun is plainly seen to boil and burst
> Too horribly for hell.
> So, judging from these two,
> As we must do,
> The Universe, outside our living Earth,
> Was all conceiv'd in the Creator's mirth,
> Forecasting at the time Man's spirit deep,
> To make dirt cheap,
> Put by the Telescope!
> Better without it man may see,
> Stretch'd awful in the hush'd midnight,

The ghost of his eternity.
Give me the nobler glass that swells to the eye
The things which near us lie,
Till Science rapturously hails,
In the minutest water-drop,
A torment of innumerable tails.
These at the least do live.

He exults with equal vigour when even dead matter
turns out to be full of furious atomic energy.

But for compulsion of strong grace,
The Pebble in the road
Would straight explode,
And fill the ghastly boundlessness of space.
The furious power,
To soft growth twice constrain'd in leaf and flower,
Protests, and longs to flash its faint self far
Beyond the dimmest star.

There are also, unfortunately, childish gibes at
Jews and Protestants. There is more of Patmore's
Turk-like anti-feminism, as where the Sibyl explains
to Psyche—

Her wedlock's marr'd when either's miss'd:
Or when she's kiss'd, but beaten not,
Or duly beaten, but not kiss'd.

But this wayward metre of *The Unknown Eros*, with
its irregular lines and rhymes, suits its wayward poet
like a swinging Spanish cloak; where the kid-gloved
style of the *Angel* often became grotesque.

And when Patmore is not being wayward but

simply human, his new style can lend itself admirably,
as in *The Azalea*.

There, where the sun shines first
Against our room,
She train'd the gold Azalea, whose perfume
She, Spring-like, from her breathing grace dispersed.
Last night the delicate crests of saffron bloom,
For this their dainty likeness watch'd and nurst,
Were just at point to burst.
At dawn I dream'd, O God, that she was dead,
And groan'd aloud upon my wretched bed,
And waked, ah God, and did not waken her,
But lay, with eyes still closed,
Perfectly bless'd in the delicious sphere
By which I knew so well that she was near,
My heart to speechless thankfulness composed.
Till 'gan to stir
A dizzy somewhat in my troubled head—
It *was* the Azalea's breath, and she *was* dead!

The fatuous vanity of the author of the *Angel* has
hardened now into a less complacent pride.

Therefore no 'plaint be mine
Of listeners none,
No hope of render'd use or proud reward,
In hasty times and hard;
But chants as of a lonely thrush's throat
At latest eve,
That does in each calm note
Both joy and grieve;
Notes few and strong and fine,
Gilt with sweet day's decline,
And sad with promise of a different sun.

94

> 'Mid the loud concert harsh
> Of this fog-folded marsh,
> To me, else dumb,
> Uranian Clearness, come!
> Give me to breathe in peace and in surprise
> The light-thrill'd ether of your rarest skies.

That prayer was not unheard. Similarly he has discarded his too facile optimism for a far more bracing bitterness.

> Here, in this little Bay,
> Full of tumultuous life and great repose,
> Where, twice a day,
> The purposeless, glad ocean comes and goes,
> Under high cliffs, and far from the huge town,
> I sit me down.
> For want of me the world's course will not fail:
> When all its work is done, the lie shall rot;
> The truth is great, and shall prevail,
> When none cares whether it prevail or not.

At this point Patmore would have been wise to stop writing. But in 1878 he published *Amelia*, which is indeed in the same free metre as *The Unknown Eros*, but relapses badly into the manner of *The Angel*. Here the poet of fifty-five imagines himself taking a young lady called Amelia, on whom he has honourable designs, to visit the grave of another young lady called Millicent, whom, needless to say, he had been going to marry, had not death saved her.

"Amelia" says one luminous verse, "Amelia had more luck than Millicent." Perhaps?

While, therefore, now
Her pensive footstep stirr'd
The darnell'd garden of unheedful death,
She ask'd what Millicent was like, and heard
Of eyes like her's, and honeysuckle breath,
And of a wiser than a woman's brow,
Yet fill'd with only woman's love, and how
An incidental greatness character'd
Her unconsider'd ways.
But all my praise
Amelia thought too slight for Millicent,
And on my lovelier-freighted arm she leant,
For more attent;
And the tea-rose I gave,
To deck her breast, she dropp'd upon the grave.
"And this was her's", said I, decoring with a band
Of mildest pearls Amelia's milder hand.
"Nay, I will wear it for *her* sake", she said:
For dear to maidens are their rivals dead.

You never know when this sentimentalist will suddenly turn cynic.

Mary Annish and mad-dog by turns, Patmore has left perhaps a dozen or twenty pages that will live. Too many of his roses are "tea-roses". But he *was* a poet, though except at magnificent moments a minor one—smaller, I feel, than his own disciple Francis Thompson. To me his character is really more interesting than his poetry. For I love eccentrics—more power to their elbows! "I have respected posterity", wrote Patmore, "and should there be a posterity that cares for letters I dare to hope that it will respect me." It will, I think—even if it smiles a little.

Francis Thompson thought him the greatest poet of the century; but that is mere idolatry. Arnold called him "that worthy, but mildish author". *The Angel* is certainly "mildish"; but not *The Unknown Eros*. That seems too severe.

The late Professor Housman had no undue "respect" for literary reputations. But I was pleased to find in the recent memoir of him a view of Patmore which seems to me truer, though a little too kind— "Nobody admires his best poetry enough, though the stupid Papists may fancy they do." "But," Housman adds, "I should say as little as possible about his nasty mixture of piety and concupiscence."

VI

DANTE GABRIEL ROSSETTI

Tous ces grands artistes brûlent la chandelle par les deux bouts: il leur faut une existence dévergondée qui excite un peu l'imagination. Mais ils meurent à l'hôpital, parce qu'ils n'ont pas eu l'esprit, étant jeunes, de faire des économies.

MONSIEUR HOMAIS, in *Madame Bovary*.

One evening in the year 1821 a couple of English subalterns knocked at a door in Naples. They vanished within and a little later reappeared with a third figure, also in British regimentals, who got into a carriage with them and drove away. In that moment Italy was giving something to repay England's loss when, in the very next year, the waters of the Gulf of Spezzia closed over Shelley's head. The figure in disguise was Gabriele Rossetti, the son of a blacksmith in the Abruzzi; a boy of promise, he had been sent to the University of Naples, then become a museum-official there and a writer of libretti for operas. In 1820 he took part in a rising which extorted a constitution from Ferdinand I; in 1821 Ferdinand, backed by Austrian cannon, stamped out his own constitution and proscribed the Liberals. Rossetti's escape was arranged, as described, by the sympathy of the wife of the British admiral in Naples Harbour; it seems a very odd proceeding, both from a diplomatic and a naval point of view; but it added to the roll of English poets the children born a few years later to the exile in London, Dante Gabriel and Christina Rossetti.

Twenty-seven years after, in 1848, while a new train of revolutions was exploding across Europe, three young men in a house in Gower St. sat planning a little revolution of their own. Their names were William Holman Hunt, John Millais, and Dante Gabriel Rossetti. They were painters and the eldest was only twenty-one. But for all that their revolution was to be more successful than most. It was wanted.

The nineteenth century had reached middle-age. There was a feeling in the air of exhaustion and stagnation. Painting in particular was dominated by the Royal Academy; and the Royal Academy was dominated by Raphael. Raphael had a habit of arranging his figures pyramidally, on a ground-line describing a letter S, with the highest light on the principal figure; therefore all young painters, as they loved their livelihood, must learn to arrange their figures pyramidally, on a ground-line describing the letter S, with the highest light on the principal figure. There was no appeal. To quote Ruskin: "We begin, in all probability, by telling the youth of fifteen or sixteen that Nature is full of faults and that he is to improve her: but that Raphael is perfect and the more he copies Raphael, the better: that after much copying of Raphael he is to try what he can do himself in a Raphaelesque but yet original manner: that is to say, he is to try to do something very clever all out of his own head, but yet this clever something is to be properly subjected to Raphaelesque rules". Poetry was less cramped; but here too Tennyson had already become a sort of Raphael, and bestrode a world in which there seemed no new thing left to do.

It was in painting that the revolt began. On that evening in 1848 was founded the Pre-Raphaelite Brotherhood, which came to consist of Hunt, Millais, Rossetti, and four others. Their main principle was a return to Nature; most artistic revolutions are, indeed, returns to Nature. That is itself very natural. A great artist arises; he forms a school and a style; the style stiffens into a formula, a "soulless self-reflection of man's skill"; until at last a new generation blazes into revolt and "returns to Nature". These young men wanted to get back from formulae to truth, from vague generalizations to seeing things vividly and minutely. They wanted something less idealized than Raphael; they found it in the simpler sincerity of the Italian painters before him; hence their name. That was all.

There seems little in all this to upheave society from its foundations. And yet no sooner was the existence of the Brotherhood betrayed by an indiscretion of Rossetti's, than pandemonium was let loose. The young Pre-Raphaelites were denounced by their frightened and infuriated elders as monsters of conceit, affectation, hideousness, obscenity, and blasphemy. Dickens thundered in *Household Words*; Charles

Kingsley pronounced their ideals worthy of "a petri-
fied Cyclops"; clergymen wrote pamphlets prophesy-
ing "Woe, woe, woe to exceedingly young men of
stubborn instincts calling themselves Pre-Raphaelites";
and it was only the entrance of Ruskin into the battle
with two letters to *The Times* that turned the struggle
in their favour. The frenzies died away; the young
painters themselves followed diverging paths; the
Brotherhood dropped to pieces; and in after-years
Rossetti would be irritated by people's interest in it.
"Madam", he said once, "I am not an -ite of any
sort: I am only a painter." That was true; but for all
that the movement left its mark both on painting and
poetry.

In poetry, too, the essential idea of the Pre-
Raphaelites, as expressed in a short-lived paper they
founded, called *The Germ*, was a return to sincerity
and simplicity—a simplicity sometimes mediaeval,
sometimes also mystical, a love of little things and of
beauty drawn in as simply as the breath.

> Our mother rose from where she sat:
> Her needles, as she laid them down,
> Met lightly, and her silken gown
> Settled; no other noise than that.

It is like the utterance of a child, naïve in its language
and with a child's fresh perception of sights and
sounds as slight as the tiny chink of needles laid aside;

and yet it is not really childish at all, being highly
sophisticated underneath. It recalls the fresh, cold
air of autumn mornings, white with dew, which are
so like spring, and yet profoundly different.

But the spring-like freshness does not last. Christina
Rossetti indeed did keep this style throughout her
life; she was the truest Pre-Raphaelite of them all;
but with her brother, and William Morris and still
more with Swinburne, it was only a dawning phase.
In Dante Gabriel Rossetti the autumn morning gives
place to the brooding, sultry, thunderous heat of an
autumn afternoon; an atmosphere that some find
stifling, but that few forget.

The outline of his life all know—how he fell in love
with Lizzie Siddal, the daughter of a Sheffield trades-
man, a pallid, grey-eyed, auburn, consumptive beauty,
with a strange gift of her own for drawing and
writing like a born Pre-Raphaelite; how after ten
years they were married, and two years later still,
sick and unhappy and realizing that she had been
married in the end for duty, not for love, she poisoned
herself with laudanum; how in an agony of remorse
he buried his poems in her coffin, between her cheek
and hair; how they lay under the earth of Highgate
seven years, until they were raised again from beside
that still perfect face and given to the world; how
amid the praise that greeted them rose one voice,

Robert Buchanan's, denouncing Rossetti as a satyr
and a sensualist; how, shaken already by insomnia
and chloral, his mind now gave way till he thought
the world leagued against him, and the very thrushes
singing in his garden put there by his enemies to drive
him mad; how he was nursed back to a sort of health
for ten years more of painting and poetry till he died
at Birchington in 1882.

He is a sombre figure, the Rossetti of the closing
years—this eccentric, passionate, heavy-featured
Italian, so handsome once, now vainly rapping
tables to recall his dead wife's spirit, or tossing sleepless in the gloom of that lonely room in Cheyne Walk,
black and stifling with its velvet curtains and old oak;
while outside in the garden stirred uneasily in their
slumber the strange beasts he had gathered there,
wombats and marmots and racoons and armadillos,
ravens and owls and chameleons and salamanders, a
perfect Goblin Market of them. And yet to the last
there remained something imperial about him, like a
falling Caesar alone in his capital; his old friends he had
estranged—Ruskin, Madox Brown, William Morris;
yet his personality, his power, the wit that flashed
across his gloom, still conquered others. There was a
greatness about him. That is not a quality for which
much space is usually found in modern biographies.
It is not amusing. But it was there.

DANTE GABRIEL ROSSETTI

The same transition from autumn dawn to autumn
afternoon marks both Rossetti's painting and his
poetry. Just as in his life the pale face of Lizzie
Siddal gave place to the full-flushed beauty of Fanny
Cornforth, so in his pictures the bright girlhood of
Mary Virgin yielded to the dark and brooding beauty
of Proserpine, in his verse the Blessed Damozel was
replaced by the Siren who stands waiting in the
apple-boughs above the pit of dead men's bones in
that grim poem left unfinished when he died:

Piled deep below the screening apple-branch,
  They lie with bitten apples in their hands:
And some are only ancient bones that blanch,
And some had ships that last year's wind did launch,
  And some were yesterday the lords of lands.

In the soft dell, among the apple-trees,
  High up above the hidden pit she stands,
And there for ever sings, who gave to these,
That lie below, her magic hour of ease,
  And those her apples holden in their hands.

Rossetti knew well the place and the Siren and the
apple: he had himself tasted it. What a change indeed
between his first state and his last! Early and late,
his work casts, somehow, a spell: but in the later
years his white magic has turned into black. Yet,
after all, with a little wisdom after the event we
can see now how natural a change it was. Indeed,
we may wonder whether those who screeched so

grotesquely at the young Pre-Raphaelites in 1850, were not by some dim instinct wiser in their generation than they knew. For rebels like Arnold and Mill and George Eliot were rebels only of the intellect, fighting for freedom of thought; but behind this young Italian lay a rebellion of the senses, a war of liberation of the passions. He might paint white Virgins with lilies; we can see now how those lilies were to fester, how from that Virgin were in the end to spring the Dolores of Swinburne and the Salome of Oscar Wilde. This warm breath from the South, fluttering the aspidistras and muslin curtains of the Victorians, was the forerunner of a gale that has blown their padded domesticity inside out by now; and when in 1870 Rossetti's poems rose to life from that grave at Highgate, and the Prussian batteries closed in around Sedan, the first cracks were spreading further in the foundations of that snug Victorian world. For Rossetti was part of a larger movement than his own —the return of paganism, the unchaining of Dionysus; and his triumph and his despair were both alike in the nature of things—his triumph, because the Victorians were trying to shut their eyes to a side of life that will not be denied; and the sadness of his despair, because with the beauty of the senses that he pursued—

How passionately and irretrievably,
In what fond flight how many ways and days!—

there comes also this shattering sense of transience and decay. It cannot be helped; a passionate sensitiveness to beauty has to be paid for, like everything else; it is a Love that walks hand in hand with Death. No race has felt that passion more intensely than the Greeks; and none has felt more intensely the bitterness of time. They did not write, in the style of Browning's *Rabbi ben Ezra*, amiable ditties about the blessings of old age.

> These arms are like the twisted thorn,
> And yet there beauty lay—

before that cry of a modern poet one feels that there are things for which the cant of consolation is an outrage.

And so it was natural that Rossetti, who had, I think, a passion for the loveliness of life more violent than any English poet, even Keats, should so soon exchange his youthful freshness for this brooding, haunted sense of lost days and vanished hours, that he saw standing like phantoms before him, "sleepless, with cold commemorative eyes". What wonder if he felt it doubly, when among those phantoms lurked also the lost face of Lizzie Siddal?

> There is a change in every hour's recall,
> And the last cowslip in the field we see
> On the same day with the first corn-poppy:
> Alas for hourly change! Alas for all
> The Loves that from his hand proud Youth lets fall
> Even as the beads of a told rosary!

*   *   *   *

What whisperest thou? Nay, why
Name the dead hours? I mind them well.
Their ghosts in many darkened doorways dwell
With desolate eyes to know them by.

"Tears, idle tears"—but these taste bitterer than
Tennyson's. Year by year, as Rossetti thus broods
upon the past, his whole tone grows dreamier, his
pictures darker and fleshlier, his verse exchanges its
first bell-like sound for the organ-roll of long Latin
words, that roll thundering onward like some Mass
sung for the dead.

Ah! who shall dare to search through what sad
maze
Thenceforth their incommunicable ways
Follow the desultory feet of Death?

*　　　*　　　*　　　*

O love, my love, if I no more should see
Thyself, nor on the earth the shadow of thee,
Nor image of thine eyes in any spring—
How then should sound upon Life's darkening slope
The ground-whirl of the perished leaves of Hope,
The wind of Death's imperishable wing!

He comes at such times to seem the lotus-eater of an
eternal afternoon; his chloral brought him no such
dreams as opium brings, but like his idol Coleridge,
Rossetti too has a dream-world of his own, with a
vividness about it that can be almost terrifying—he
too became

DANTE GABRIEL ROSSETTI

>Master of the murmuring courts,
>   Where the shapes of sleep convene.

But Rossetti had the passions, as well as the dreaminess, of the South; he could depict them as neither Tennyson nor Arnold could; and the terrible brevities of *Sister Helen,* as she melts before the destroying flame the waxen image of her false lover, brought back into English poetry a stark intensity of feeling that had not been there since the Elizabethan dramatists; though the formalized stab and counter-stab of its dialogue recall, rather, ancient tragedy.

>"He sends a ring and a broken coin,
>   Sister Helen,
>And bids you mind the banks of Boyne."
>"What else he broke will he ever join,
>   Little brother?"
>   (*O Mother, Mary Mother,*
>*No, never joined, between Hell and Heaven!*)

>"He yields you these and craves full fain,
>   Sister Helen,
>You pardon him in his mortal pain."
>"What else he took will he give again,
>   Little brother?"
>   (*O Mother, Mary Mother,*
>*Not twice to give, between Hell and Heaven.*)

Indeed, if much of Rossetti's poetry has about it a touch of the lotus-eater, it is only fair to remember that none the less its author in some measure worked himself to death, and spent on the attainment of final perfection a labour untiring and ungrudged; it would have been well if Browning, who complained of Rossetti's "effeminacy", had expended on his own productions one half of that "fundamental brainwork" on which Rossetti insisted in all poetry. "Effeminate" the work of this strange tormented man may sometimes seem; but those who find him so, should open his works at the poem he wrote in his last illness, *The King's Tragedy*. It is as if he had there turned finally from the vain repinings of Southern tenderness to that simple courage of the North which finds, like Arnold, the only remedy, not in any vain comforts, but in endurance of what must be endured. That tale of the death of James I of Scotland stands, like *Sister Helen*, in the front rank of English ballads. Never did Rossetti's power of grim atmosphere and sinister symbolism show itself stronger or bolder than in this vision of violent death, traced by a dying hand.

> And the woman held his eyes with her eyes:—
> "O King, thou art come at last;
> But thy wraith has haunted the Scottish Sea
> To my sight for four years past.
>
> "Four years it is since first I met,
> 'Twixt the Duchray and the Dhu,
> A shape whose feet clung close in a shroud,
> And that shape for thine I knew.

"A year again, and on Inchkeith Isle
　　I saw thee pass in the breeze,
With the cerecloth risen above thy feet
　　And wound about thy knees.

"And yet a year, in the Links of Forth,
　　As a wanderer without rest,
Thou cam'st with both thine arms i'the shroud
　　That clung high up thy breast.

"And in this hour I find thee here,
　　And well mine eyes may note
That the winding-sheet hath passed thy breast
　　And risen around thy throat."

Or again, in a last passage of supreme symbolism—

And the rain had ceased, and the moonbeams lit
　　The window high in the wall,—
Bright beams that on the plank I knew
　　Through the painted pane did fall,
And gleamed with the splendour of Scotland's crown
　　And shield armorial.

But then a great wind swept up the skies
　　And the climbing moon fell aback;
And the royal blazon fled from the floor,
　　And nought remained on its track;
And high in the darkened window-pane
　　The shield and the crown were black.

Rossetti's is not a gay life to contemplate. He was
terribly unhappy; and that the Pecksniffs and Pod-
snaps can never forgive. But after all, as the Japanese

proverb says, "It is better to be a crystal and be broken, than to be perfect like the tile upon the house-top". The crystal that was Rossetti, came to a shattered end; but the visions that found life there, live still. Like Blake, he was poet and painter in one; and like Blake he saw the world ablaze with all its colours, not as a colour-blind pattern of moral blacks and whites. The English writers of his age tended to have too much conscience and too little artistic conscience: he was needed. Through him, this "great Italian", as Ruskin called him, "tormented in the inferno of London", Italy gave to the England of Tennyson what she had given before to the England of Chaucer and, again, of Shakespeare, a sense of beauty, naked and not ashamed. Life denied him much, gave him much only to take it back again; his fate may seem a failure and a tragedy; yet in words of his own, that might serve for his epitaph, he has recorded all the hopes he cared or dared to cherish—and those at least were not in vain:

> Crave thou no dower of earthly things
> Unworthy Hope's imaginings;
> To have brought true birth of Song to be
> And to have won hearts to Poesy,
> Or anywhere in the sun or rain
> To have loved and been beloved again,
> Is loftiest reach of Hope's bright wings.

VII

CHRISTINA ROSSETTI

"Au trait qui me navra de ta grâce enfantine."
RONSARD

"The worst of it is", says the late Sir Walter Raleigh in one of his letters, "that you cannot lecture on really pure poetry, any more than you can talk about the ingredients of pure water." (Sir Walter was clearly no scientist.) "It is adulterated, methylated, sanded poetry that makes the best lectures." (No doubt he is thinking of poets like Browning, Meredith, or the Metaphysicals.) "The only thing Christina makes me want to do is cry, not lecture." That, surely, is the effect any true poet would wish to produce. And the only excuse for lecturing on her is that many still do not know, because she wrote much depressing verse on a depressing creed, how good her best can be.

Christina Rossetti's poetry is so poignant partly because it seems the cry of a soul from some far simpler age, as lost amid Victorian industrialism as a wood-dove in a factory. Her brother and Morris and Swinburne were moderns seeking inspiration in the mediaeval; she seems, rather, a mediaeval wraith shrinking in shy dismay before the harsh babel of modernity. In the Age of Steam she remained like some quiet anchoress of the Age of Faith—one who might have sat to Giotto, or knelt before St Francis at Assisi. Born out of due time, she came to sit instead like Dante's "La Pia" in her brother's picture, waiting for the grey death that crept mistily nearer across the feverish Maremma of that London where she lived exiled.

Her refugee father, Gabriele Rossetti, had married in England a bride half Italian by blood, but strongly Anglican by creed. Her religion she transmitted to her two daughters, Maria and Christina, born in 1827 and 1830. That faith was to mould their fate.

Maria indeed exerted a deep influence on her younger sister; not altogether a happy influence, if we may believe Gosse, who compares it to the unfortunate hold of the fanatical ex-slaver Newton on the imaginative Cowper. Christina herself records with admiration that Maria would not look at Blake's illustrations to *Job*, as being a breach of the Commandment against graven images; nor visit the Mummyroom at the British Museum, because it would be so fearful if the Resurrection occurred while one was there. And when Maria died in a sisterhood in 1876, once more Christina comments: "The dear thing's readiness was such that it would need an act of resignation on her part to resign herself to life."

But Christina herself remained less placidly acquiescent—

Alas, no saint rejoicing in her bed.

Hers was a more passionate heart; and if she was mediaeval in her childlike faith, she was mediaeval also in her horrified obsession with the grave. As a child, she once found a dead mouse and buried it; then a few days later she went to look and sickened at what she found. Often indeed the childhood of poets contains some such symbolic incident that foreshadows their whole future. The years were to come when Christina Rossetti seemed to see a dead mouse under every sod.

But here appears already another trait that she shared with Dante Gabriel—a passion for animals, which got her bitten at six years old by a peccary in Regent's Park and at forty-five could still make her write gaily to her brother William: "Bristol, by the bye, looks a picturesque town; and I find there is a local Zoo." The strange creatures of *Goblin Market* mustered early in Christina's imagination.

> One had a cat's face,
> One whisked a tail,
> One tramped at a rat's pace,
> One crawled like a snail,
> One like a wombat prowled obtuse and furry,
> One like a ratel tumbled hurry skurry.

Had she indeed, one wonders, a secret, unconfessed envy of the beasts that perish, unvexed by anguished memories, untormented by conscience, unterrified by the menace of eternity?—like poor Cowper fondling his hares on the brink of the undying flame? She would have sympathised with that healthy old barbarian, Walt Whitman, crying—

"I think I could turn and live with the animals;
they are so placid and self-contained."

Though she would never, never have dared, like
him, to continue—

They do not lie awake in the dark and weep for their
  sins,
They do not make me sick discussing their duty to
  God.

Her poetry too came early, with promise both of
her future gifts and of her unhappiness. Already the
scene is laid for the conflict between the two selves
in her soul. For the frail yet indomitable young saint
who looks from her brother's pictures of the Girlhood
of Mary Virgin and of the Annunciation was to
subject year by year to ever harsher martyrdom the
more human, humorous Christina who loved children, and furry wombats, and the calling of gay
Goblin-men from the twilit market of forbidden
things.

Before the age of six, before she could even write,
she was chanting—

Cecilia never went to school
Without her gladiator.

But a gladiator was what Christina never found. Alas
that both Mr Collinson and Mr Cayley were to show
in their make-up so singularly little of the gladia-
torial!

CHRISTINA ROSSETTI

The same whimsicality recurs in lines written at fourteen:

> The roses lingered in her cheeks,
> When fair Albina fainted.
> O gentle reader, could it be
> That fair Albina fainted?

Unfortunately, as years passed her health grew as delicate as her style. And her conscience as delicate as her health.

"Soon you will be too polite to live with", groaned her brother William when she was seventeen. She gave up chess, because it makes you wish to beat your opponent; she gave up the theatre, because actors are often not all they should be. Renunciation fills her poems—*Love Ephemeral; Burial Anthem, The Dead Bride, The Dying Man to his Betrothed.* No doubt it is common enough for seventeen to write as gloomily as if it were seventy-seven. At the same age the young Tennyson was choosing subjects like *The Vale of Bones*. But usually the young grow out of it: Christina did not. It was with her no mere affectation, "melancholy as night for wantonness". She was not one of those brooding owls that are really young peacocks in disguise. Hers is the cry of a sensitive spirit, not only persecuted by conscience, but also sadly lacking in vitality and wearing its young life already as a burden, not as an unfolding flower.

Even in childhood oft my spirit sank,
Thinking of all that still had to be done.

At nineteen she is already as weary as if she had
lived for an age; though as tuneful as if she had
written for one.

> Where sunless rivers weep
> Their waves into the deep,
> She sleeps a charmèd sleep:
>   Awake her not.
> Led by a single star,
> She came from very far
> To seek where shadows are
>   Her pleasant lot.
>
> Rest, rest, a perfect rest,
> Shed over brow and breast;
> Her face is toward the west,
>   The purple land.
> She cannot see the grain
> Ripening on hill and plain,
> She cannot feel the rain
>   Upon her hand.

No striking ideas, no startling imagery: merely
pure poetry.

Stranger still, this gifted, hag-ridden girl is already
obsessed, as if by premonition, with the falsity and
vanity of all earthly love. "Character", it has been
said, "is destiny": it seems no more than the simple
truth to the reader of these poems written before
ever James Collinson or Charles Cayley came to

break her heart—or to have it broken over them.
This passionate soul was self-doomed to sorrow.

> I sought among the living and I seek
>   Among the dead, for some to love; but few
>   I found at last, and those had quite run through
> Their store of love; and friendship is too weak,
> Too cold for me; yet will I never speak,
>   Telling my heart-want to smooth listeners who
>   Would wonder smiling; I can bear and do—
> Hot shame shall dry no tears upon my cheek.
> So when my dust shall mix with other dust,
>   When I shall have found quiet in decay,
>   And lie at ease and cease like a mere thought—
>   Those whom I loved, thinking on me, shall not
> Grieve with a measure, saying, "Now we must
>   Weep for a little ere we laugh to-day."

That typical cry of bitterness was written at eighteen,
to *bouts rimés*, as a game.

In the autumn of this same troubled 1848 Christina
Rossetti fell in love with a young Pre-Raphaelite,
James Collinson. He was a little dormouse of a man
who was always falling asleep, even in front of models
at a shilling an hour, and always having jokes played
by his friends upon his somnolence. Under the influence of Cardinal Wiseman he had been converted
to Rome; under the influence of Christina he reverted
to Anglicanism; and they became engaged. But in
1850 his sleepy conscience woke with a start and back
he went to Rome. "Indomitable in her feebleness",

she broke off her engagement; though, meeting him near Regent's Park soon afterwards, she fainted. It had not been easy.

From House to Home recalls that ordeal. It is in the metre of Tennyson's *Dream of Fair Women*. But what does borrowed metre matter to real originality? The voice is the voice of Christina Rossetti alone.

> That night destroyed me like an avalanche;
> One night turned all my summer back to snow:
> Next morning not a bird upon my branch,
> Not a lamb woke below...
>
> Azure and sun were starved from heaven above,
> No dew had fallen but biting frost lay hoar.
> O love, I knew that I should meet my love,
> Should find my love no more...
>
> Then with a cry like famine I arose
> I lit my candle, searched from room to room,
> Searched up and down; a war of winds that froze
> Swept through the blank of gloom...
>
> These thorns are sharp, yet I can tread on them;
> This cup is loathsome, yet He makes it sweet.
> My face is steadfast towards Jerusalem,
> My heart remembers it.

Ten years passed, uneventfully (it is not the uneventful years that are easiest to bear); with a brief attempt at teaching, much domesticity, a steady, unnoticed flow of poetry.

CHRISTINA ROSSETTI

> Underneath the growing grass,
>> Underneath the living flowers,
>> Deeper than the sound of showers;
>> There we shall not count the hours
> By the shadows as they pass.

Always the "shadows"! She was indeed a human sundial, casting a shadow on all her days.

> None know the choice I made: I make it still.
>> None know the choice I made and broke my heart,
> Breaking mine idol: I have braced my will,
>> Once, chosen for once my part.

And again—

> I dwell alone—I dwell alone, alone,
>> Whilst full my river flows down to the sea,
> Gilded with flashing boats
>> That bring no friend to me;
> O love-songs gurgling from a hundred throats,
>> O love-pangs, let me be.

Amid diction otherwise so perfect and unforced, "gurgling" is not a very happy word. It suggests an Aristophanic chorus of frogs. Did poor Christina, maddened by a happiness she could not share, choose it, unconsciously, for that very reason—to express her sardonic bitterness? For the "gay, uncmbittered lips" of Sara Teasdale's fine ambition were (who shall blame her?) not to be hers.

But in the same year as this last piece, 1858, she wrote another, which has become famous and was the first to make her so—*Uphill.*

Does the road wind up-hill all the way?
  Yes, to the very end.
Will the day's journey take the whole long day?
  From morn to night, my friend.

But is there for the night a resting-place?
  A roof for when the slow dark hours begin
May not the darkness hide it from my face?
  You cannot miss that inn.

Here is something more sinister than the melo-dramatic flesh-creepings of Edgar Allan Poe. For the true triumph of the gruesome imagination is to employ familiar things, just a little changed till they become horrible—more horrible than things completely strange; in the same way as it is worse to be stabbed by a loved hand than by one unknown. Here is something grimmer than any "ghoul-haunted woodlands of Weir". It is the old device of the Anglo-Saxon *Grave-poem*—"for thee was a house built, ere that thou born wert". But its force is not enfeebled by its age.

In 1861 *Uphill* appeared in *Macmillan's Magazine* and made an impression: next year with her volume *Goblin Market and other Poems*, despite Ruskin's disapproving forebodings, Christina Rossetti won the first literary victory of the Pre-Raphaelites—"the Jael of our movement" Swinburne called her. But, alas, Christina was no Jael; it was in her own flesh that she hammered home the nails.

CHRISTINA ROSSETTI

Charles Bagot Cayley was a stock type of gentle, absent, unworldly scholar—a translator of Homer and Dante into English (whence he had been a pupil of Christina's father), and even of the *New Testament* into Iroquois. Dante Gabriel's letters contain ribald references to him as "the great unshaved" and "a fair type of Divine Comedy"; and it is recorded that he finally broke an anguished silence in the presence of two fashionable ladies at a party with the hopeful question—"Are you interested in the Gulf Stream?" Accordingly it seems to have taken this gentle owl some time to discover that Christina was interested in him.

> The blindest buzzard that I know
>   Does not wear wings to spread and stir;
>   Nor does my special mole wear fur,
> And grub away the roots below:
> He sports a tail indeed, but then
> It's to a coat: he's man with men:
>   His quill is cut to a pen...
>
> My blindest buzzard that I know,
>   My special mole, when will you see?
>   O no, you must not look at me,
> There's nothing hid for me to show
> I might show facts as plain as day:
> But since your eyes are blind, you'd say,
>   "Where? What?" and turn away.

Once more, as so often, Christina takes refuge in her dear animal world, which she found kindlier than

that of men. But there are other poems where even
this show of gaiety breaks down—

> You took my heart in your hand
> With a friendly smile,
> With a critical eye you scanned,
> Then set it down,
> And said: It is still unripe,
> Better wait awhile;
> Wait while the skylarks pipe,
> Till the corn grows brown.
> As you set it down it broke—

And yet it would seem unfair to poor Mr Cayley
not to see in Christina herself a bent towards self-
torture. For at last he did propose. But then (why
not sooner?) came the question of his beliefs. He
was an agnostic. And so—in spite of her brother
William's pleadings—all was over. They could only
go on meeting as friends, until Cayley's death in 1882
wrung from her the dirge that begins—

> Unmindful of the roses,
> Unmindful of the thorn,
> A reaper tired reposes
> Among his gathered corn.
> So might I, till the morn!

Too little known are the passionate Italian poems,
Il Rosseggiar dell' Oriente, also occasioned by the same
unhappy love.

This great refusal came in 1866, the year of her
Prince's Progress, with its recurrence to her constant
theme of love left lonely until too late. The rest of

her life is a grey record of piety, poetry, bereavement, and sickness, till in 1894 she died of cancer; tortured in mind also, like poor Cowper, with doubts of her salvation.

Tantum religio potuit suadere malorum.

So, simple in mind to the last as a novice in a nunnery, though so passionate at heart, there passed away this strange, pathetic figure who would not step on a piece of paper in the street lest it should be written with the name of God; and changed the name of a devotional work of hers from *Nowhere* to *Speaking Likenesses*, because she had heard of a free-thinking work called *Erewhon*; and tormented herself with the reproach that her good deeds were done not from Christian love, but self-respect; and found edification in such incredibly naive moral stories as that of the lady who consoled herself for the largeness of her feet by the reflection that all the more people could borrow her boots. The pity of it all is not lessened—it is heightened—by the courage with which this lonely, ailing, and ageing woman could still laugh at herself. "If only my figure would shrink somewhat; for a fat poetess is incongruous, especially when seated by the grave of buried hope." If she jested at her scars, it was not because the wounds had not been felt. And they were not felt the less, for being so largely self-inflicted.

When it becomes tyrannical, the thing once called

"the conscience" and now "the super-ego" can turn into as terrible a scourge as other dictators. The fate of Christina Rossetti is a thing to shudder at—this life, in her own phrase, "pared down and subdued and repressed to an intolerable level". But what were the effects on her poetry?

First, the ill effects. They are obvious. "Vanity of vanities" is a theme that has produced great poetry, both before and since *Ecclesiastes*: but it easily grows wearisome; in her own words—

> Gravely monotonous like a passing bell.

You may (to quote her again)—

> Say of laughter it is vain,
> Of mirth, what profits it?

But, after all, what profits so much lamentation, either? You may—

> sit mourning like a mournful owl
> And like a doleful dragon make ado.

But your hearers are liable, after a little while, to slip softly away.

The grief of great tragedy is not depressing. It is too rammed with vitality. There, even in the midst of death we are in life.

> Terrify babes, my Lord, with painted devils.
> I am past such needlesse palsy.

But it is a far cry from that defiance of Vittoria Corombona's to Christina Rossetti, whose passive suffering grows as unbearable to contemplate as a child being tortured and pleading pitifully only to be left in peace.

> O earth, lie heavily upon her eyes;
> Seal her sweet eyes, weary of watching, Earth;
> Lie close around her; leave no room for mirth
> With its harsh laughter, nor for sound of sighs.

Indeed there was a tendency for most laughter to seem harsh to her. "I am afraid", writes Dante Gabriel to her, "you find art interferes with the legitimate exercise of anguish." "All the comic side of Shakespeare", records her other brother, William Michael, "—except some bits of simple 'fun', such as Dogberry and Verges—was certain to be distasteful to her.... Sir Toby Belch and Falconbridge would simply repel her, and even Falstaff would find little indulgence and elicit only watery smiles."

Further, this prisoned life of abnegation does lead at times to a certain waspish hatred of others' happiness, which becomes as unpleasant as her own unhappiness is pitiful. At such moments she grows, in Webster's superb phrase, "too full of choler with living honest".

> Sweetness of beauty moved me to despair,
> Stung me to anger by its mere content.

She acquires, instead, a fish-like taste for worms.

The paling roses of a cloud,
  The fading bow that arches space,
These woo my fancy towards my shroud,
    Towards the place
  Of faces veiled, of heads discrowned and bowed.

How far from Wordsworth, whose heart a rainbow
in the sky made to leap, not to think of shrouds!
Even for the Bible the rainbow was a promise; for
Christina Rossetti, it becomes a threat.

Or again:

There are a hundred subtle stings
    To prick us in our daily walk:
    A young fruit cankered on its stalk,
  A strong bird snared for all his wings,
  A nest that sang but never sings:
  Yea, sight and sound and silence stings.

"Surely the ripe fruits tremble on the bough."
How differently autumn's last red leaf danced in
its mad gaiety before the gaze of Coleridge! There
clings about this poetess a touch of that mediaeval
morbidity which delighted in Dances of Death. Per-
sistently she reverts to such themes, until she gives
at times the impression of seeing all life through the
worm-holes in a shroud. To the healthy sanity of the
Hellene this persistent wallowing in graves would
have seemed an absurd excess, paralysing and stupid.
And I hold the prejudice that, other things equal,
sane and vital poetry is better than morbid.

CHRISTINA ROSSETTI

And yet Christina Rossetti had a poetic gift that not very many have equalled. Her life was lacerated with restraint: but in literature restraint can be less harmful. The very narrowness of her real existence may have helped to intensify the force with which her imagination flowed down its one straitened outlet. Feeling intensely, she was yet intensely controlled. That, given her other gifts, helped to make her style; and it is her style, above all, that has made Christina Rossetti.

She knew far less of books, and not much more, probably, of life, than Elizabeth Barrett shuttered up in Wimpole Street; certainly she saw far less of the world than Mrs Browning, once escaped from that prison. And yet—so potent is style—most of Mrs Browning's work to-day (except for some of the *Sonnets from the Portuguese*, where the sonnet-form imposed a certain restraint that their author lacked) seems faint and faded beside Christina Rossetti's. Christina knew few things, but she knew them well; and one of them was her own mind. Reading her one remembers the words of Troilus—

> I am as true as truth's simplicity
> And simpler than the infancy of truth.

It was noticed long ago in Rome, and again in eighteenth-century France by Diderot, how often women seem spontaneously to achieve a purer style than professional scribes or grammarians. That can be seen in Sappho, in the letters of our own Dorothy Osborne, in the best verse of Mary Coleridge, Emily Dickinson, or Edna St Vincent Millay. They have escaped being educated out of their senses. "I think him clever", is Christina's verdict on some verses, "but what is the use of cleverness in matters poetic?" Quite a lot, thought the Metaphysicals; and sometimes they were right. But Christina's criticism does illustrate herself. She did not add to her own stature by taking thought; her art was a second nature. "It is something of a genuine lyric cry", she says of one of her own pieces, "and such I will back against all skilled labour."

Yet her own labour was highly "skilled"; for long practice, beginning with the *bouts rimés* of the Rossetti nursery, had given her that unconscious ease and mastery which years of writing couplets for bad plays similarly conferred on Dryden. In fact she had done what modern poets so often shirk—served out her apprenticeship.

> Hemlock groweth, poppy bloweth,
> In the fields where no man moweth.

As quietly and naturally (and often with the same touch of the sinister) her own verses grow.

> I plucked pink blossoms from mine apple-tree
> And wore them all that evening in my hair;
> Then in due season when I went to see,
> I found no apples there.

CHRISTINA ROSSETTI

It looks as easy to write like that as to pluck the blossoms: but how hard Wordsworth found it!

And yet this quiet mastery would lack its virtue if there were not also, behind it, such passion to be mastered. Under that high stiff Victorian dress with its hard collar and plain brooch there burned a need and a power to love, a rage and despair at their doomed frustration, as vehement as in Sappho or Héloïse.

When all the overwork of life
　Is finished once, and fast asleep
We swerve no more beneath the knife
　But taste that silence cool and deep;
Forgetful of the highways rough,
　Forgetful of the thorny scourge,
　Forgetful of the tossing surge,
Then shall we find it is enough?

How can we say "enough" on earth—
　"Enough" with such a craving heart?
I have not found it since my birth,
　But still have bartered part for part.

　　.　　　.　　　.　　　.　　　.

I used to labour, used to strive
　For pleasure with a restless will:
Now if I save my soul alive,
　All else what matters, good or ill?
I used to dream alone, to plan
　Unspoken hopes and days to come:—
　Of all my past this is the sum—
I will not lean on child of man.

And yet the next moment all this bitter resignation
is shattered by a fresh paroxysm of anguish.

> To give, to give, not to receive!
>   I long to pour myself, my soul,
> Not to keep back or count or leave,
>   But king with king to give the whole.
> I long for one to stir my deep—
>   I have had enough of help and gift—
>   I long for one to search and sift
> Myself, to take myself and keep.
> You scratch my surface with your pin,
>   You stroke me smooth with hushing breath:—
> Nay pierce, nay probe, nay dig within,
>   Probe my quick core and sound my depth.
> You call me with a puny call,
>   You talk, you smile, you nothing do:
>   How should I spend my heart on you,
> My heart that so outweighs you all!

It is tremendous, this instant when the meek nun's
veil is flung aside and from these lips of Christian
modesty breaks the proud and angry cry of some pagan
Medea!—even though she turns a moment later to
throw her misery, contemptuous of man, at the feet
of God.

> Not in this world of hope deferred,
>   This world of perishable stuff:
> Eye hath not seen nor ear hath heard
>   Nor heart conceived that full "enough":
> Here moans the separating sea,
>   Here harvests fail, here breaks the heart:
>   There God shall join and no man part,
> I full of Christ and Christ of me.

CHRISTINA ROSSETTI

This Mariana of Albany Street was born to have been one of the great lovers of history.

Christina Rossetti had no new ideas to give the world—only the exaggerated pietism that wrecked her own life. She was no great creator of characters. But she had one.

Four qualities I have come to value above all in the human heart—goodness, grace, gaiety, and courage. Goodness, grace, and courage were hers. For lack of a little more feather-pated gaiety her life became a thing grim to contemplate. But poetry is a thing of isolated moods: there it mattered less than in life that she wanted gaiety, seeing that she had genius. Thanks to it she still stands first among English poetesses; though for herself, it may well be, she would have been happier unborn. And so her work remains as a perfect counterpart to her brother's —beside his heady wine, her cup of pure cold water; beside his organ-roll, her silver vesper-bell; beside his Blessed Damozel, this Damozel to the end unblest.

VIII

WILLIAM MORRIS

Ce qui me semble, à moi, le plus haut dans l'Art (et le plus difficile) ce n'est ni de faire rire, ni de faire pleurer, ni de vous mettre en rut ou en fureur, mais d'agir à la façon de la nature, c'est à dire de *faire rêver*.

FLAUBERT.

"Would you like him to be a great poet?"—how many parents would jump at such an offer made by a fairy-godmother above their infant's cot! And yet—when one reads poets' biographies? Milton, Pope, Gray, Chatterton, Wordsworth, Coleridge, Shelley, Keats, Byron, Tennyson, Arnold, Rossetti, Swinburne —those figures, so often melancholy, sometimes tragic, sometimes even repellent, are not calculated to arouse much envy. We may feel it pleasanter after all to read their works than to lead their lives. I believe the average scientist is far happier. For most artists are poor masters of the art of living, and few poets have fulfilled Milton's precept of making true poems of themselves; as the Swiss guides said of Ruskin, "Le pauvre enfant, il ne sait pas vivre". Yet there are exceptions —Sophocles, perhaps (for after all we know little of him); Horace, of whom we know more; William Morris, who, thanks to himself and to one of the best biographies in English, remains vividly before us still, as a passionate, lovable being who used to the utmost the powers that genius so often squanders, in doing what he wanted to do and enjoyed doing and could do with full success; not in one art only, but in a dozen ways at once. Other writers of his century may have made more of literature; none made more of life.

Genius with him, indeed, was health, not a kind of disease: Poetry, not an anaemic avocation painfully pursued in the attic of an ivory tower, but the very atmosphere of a busy daily life. "If a chap can't compose an epic poem while he is weaving tapestry, he'd better shut up." Trollope would have understood. Morris avoided that curse of his age and ours, the divorce between brain and hand, which leaves the mechanic merely mechanical, the man of letters merely literary. For this "idle singer of an empty day" engaged successfully in painting, designing, weaving, dyeing, illuminating, printing; in making furniture, tapestry, wall-papers, stained-glass windows; in propaganda to preserve the churches of Britain, and to destroy the British Constitution—all in the intervals of writing poetry and prose that fill twenty-four volumes. "If he had started a Kelmscott Theatre", Mr Bernard Shaw has said, "instead of the Kelmscott Press, I am quite sure that in a few months, without going half a mile for his company, he would have produced work that would within ten years have affected every theatre in Europe." Making the usual allowance for the emphatic mind of Mr Bernard Shaw, we may believe it. At all events we can understand that the doctor should have diagnosed Morris's last illness as "simply being William Morris and having done more work than most ten men"; and we can

understand also the dying man's own summary—
"I have enjoyed my life—few more so".

Yet this was no facile victory of some sanguine
temperament charging through the world with eyes
too blind and a hide too thick to be aware of the
world's unhappiness. No doubt Morris's terrific
energy was partly what carried him through. He
remained a curiously elemental creature in some
ways, with his rolling gait, his look of a sea-captain,
his capacity for swearing; especially the younger
Morris, the "Topsy" whom his friends teased and
admired simultaneously, with his way of chewing
forks out of recognition, of kicking panels out of
doors, or of going and rubbing his back against them
like a sheep, when bored. But with all this horse-
power went an exceedingly clear head. Mackail's
comparison of him with Dr Johnson has provoked
loud protests; but it is less fantastic than at first might
seem. Both men, thanks to their combination of intellectual force and downright animal spirits, waged
a lifelong war on cant and unreality; and, since their
straightforward good sense would allow them no false
comforts, not even their animal spirits could save
either of them from a deep underlying sadness. Where
Morris differs most, is in having also a romantic
imagination and giving it full rein. He remains indeed
a paradox—a dreamer witched away by the glamour

of fairylands beyond space and time, and yet a realistic manual worker, now up to the elbows in dye-vats, now rioting in Trafalgar Square. Yet we can understand. If he sought the remote, it was partly because he was romantic in temper, with long-sighted eyes fixed on the blue enchantment of the distance; but it was partly because he was also realistic in temper, and nauseated in consequence by an age of unreality and pretence. It is worth remembering a snatch of conversation in *News from Nowhere*:

"You are very bitter about that unlucky nineteenth century", said I. "Naturally", said he, "since I know so much about it."

Thus Morris was doubly driven to seek escape; not out of the material world into a mystic Nowhere, but out of the Victorian Age into some period less disgusting. He moved into the time of Chaucer as one might move into the country; and he lived there with the happiness of a day-dream, but also with the precise clarity of a vision. As he once said to an interrupter at a meeting, "Young man, remember that in talking about mediaeval times I am on my own dunghill". He did not crow unduly; it was true. He took with him into the past all his sense of fact, his love of accuracy. "No man can draw armour properly unless he can draw a knight with his feet on the hob, toasting a herring on the point of his sword." He may

have idealized the Middle Ages to some extent; but
the author of *The Haystack in the Floods* never forgot
their darker side of suffering and brutality. The magic
of dream, the clarity of vision—he found them both
already in Chaucer before him:

And thou, O Master!—Yea, my Master still,
Whatever feet have scaled Parnassus hill,
Since like thy measures, clear and sweet and strong,
Thames' stream scarce fettered bore the bream along
Unto the bastioned bridge, his only chain—
O Master, pardon me if yet in vain
Thou art my Master, and I fail to bring
Before men's eyes the image of the thing
My heart is filled with: thou whose *dreamy* eyes
Beheld the flush to Cressid's cheeks arise,
When Troilus rode up the praising street,
As *clearly* as they saw thy townsmen meet
Those who in vineyards of Poictou withstood
The glittering horror of the steel-topped wood.

Being thus clear-sighted, and passionate for beauty,
and in love with life, it was inevitable that Morris
should be haunted also by the thought of beauty's
eternal fading and life's relentless end. Just as even
Chaucer had cried, with an unusual note of pain for
that gay voice of his:

Alas the wo! Alas the peines strong!...
What is this world? What axen men to have?
Now with his love, now in his colde grave,
Alone withouten any compagnie.

In consequence, Morris not only sought hungrily for life that should be worth living; he sought also for an answer to death that still remained to be died. His quest was a double one. What use to find the Earthly Paradise itself, if there too roses faded and golden locks turned grey? Hence the remote enchanted atmosphere of *The Defence of Guenevere* and *Jason*; the brooding sadness of *The Earthly Paradise*; the final change to the stoic endurance of *Sigurd the Volsung*. Thus the poetry of Morris, lovely in itself, possesses the further interest of a pilgrim's progress—a progress from the plaintive beauty of the South to the stark courage of the Icelandic North. In that world of the Saga he found at last the one consolation, that there are no consolations; that life lived hard and finely is its own reward, death its own and its only cure.

He set out early on his quest. In the hornbeam glades of Epping during the 'forties you might have met a little boy mounted on a pony and clad in a toy suit of armour—William Morris already deep in the Middle Ages. By way of Marlborough he passed to Oxford, where he met his lifelong friend, Burne-Jones. Gradually he decided to abandon the Church for Art. Inheriting nine hundred a year, he was above any need for pot-boiling. He entered an architect's office; Rossetti, whom he came to know through Burne-Jones, hypnotized him into becoming temporarily a painter; then, in 1858 appeared his first volume of verse, *The Defence of Guenevere*.

It is a remarkable first volume; not so much for its poetic merits, real as those are, as for its originality. In the evolution of most poets, as in that of the human race, there is an ape-stage, of imitation and pilfering; but of this book Swinburne's words were true: "It needed no exceptional acuteness to see that this poet held of none, stole from none, clung to none, as tenant, as beggar, or as thief". It is a work not so much of beauty as of indefinable charm. Often rude, often imperfect, it yet has the vivid appeal of certain faces that are more moving in their irregularity of feature than the conventionally handsome. It is alive. These figures out of Froissart and Malory are more real for Morris than their own living neighbours are for most people. The Guenevere who pleads with feverish incoherence against her accusers, with the flame of the stake before her, and behind her the maddening memory of the lost love that she denies and boasts alternately in her anguish and her pride; the later Guenevere who hoarsely rejects in her turn the pleadings of Lancelot, while her hand trembles on the silent tomb of Arthur severing them—how different both are from Tennyson's poor painted Queen! The comparison is indeed inevitable. The *Idylls of the King* are far more perfect in their style; they contain unforgettable pictures of land and sea; yet it always seems almost incredible that even the earliest of them (1859) should be a year later than this first volume of Morris. They appear so much more old-fashioned and less vital. It is the difference, to put it all in two lines, between Tennyson's

> Camelot, a city of shadowy palaces,

and Morris's

> The back-toll'd bells of noisy Camelot.

The same contrast makes itself between the Laureate's Sir Galahad, that Lord-Leightonish figure, with his complacent—

> My strength is as the strength of ten,
> Because my heart is pure,

and the younger poet's far more human Galahad, who endures moments of desperate yearning for the earthly passions his purity has forsworn. Again, as a picture of the Middle Ages in their grimness I know no English poem to equal *The Haystack in the Floods*. With all its technical imperfections the book contains here and there lines that haunt the memory for life:

> Edward the King is dead; at Westminster
> The carvers smooth the curls of his long beard—

(where the three long syllables that close each line seem themselves to lengthen out that flowing beard of stone); or again—

WILLIAM MORRIS

After these years the flowers forget their blood.

     *   *   *

Grim curses out of Peter and of Paul,
  Judging of strange sins in Leviticus.

     *   *   *

Up the sweep of the bridge we dashed together,
  It rocked to the crash of the meeting spears,
Down rained the buds of the dear spring weather,
  The elm-tree flowers fell like tears.

But there is one verse above all that expresses for me
the essential appeal of this first book—Guenevere's
description of her own still girlish queenliness when
first she sat upon her throne:

  My face made beautiful with my young blood.

That particular charm Morris was never quite to find
again.

His next work, *Jason* (1867), which was originally
meant to take its place in *The Earthly Paradise*, but
outgrew its frame, is a quieter, dreamier thing. The
tapestried effect he sometimes loved, makes itself felt
here in the low tones and the recurrent, conven-
tionalized imagery such as "the brown bird", "the
green billow". The rush of the poet's youth is over,
the sadness of his middle-age has not yet grown intense. When he married in 1859 and needed a home,
the hideousness of Victorian furniture had driven
him, mixture of impatient impulse and patient per-
severance that he was, to set about making everything

that he wanted, in the form that he wanted, for himself; he had founded his firm of Morris & Co., and plunged into a dozen handicrafts. *Jason* has an air of being in the same way a product, not of passionate feeling, but of happy craftsmanship. The story of the Argo, moving always, gains in his re-telling by many a happy variation here and there; and to those who ask, as some always will, "Why not in prose?", the verse itself replies by bearing the reader onward as evenly as if he were drifting down the quiet windings of the upper Thames. One song in the poem, its best remembered thing, may serve to bring back the tone and tenour of the whole.

> There comes a murmur from the shore,
> And in the place two fair streams are,
> Drawn from the purple hill afar,
> Drawn down unto the restless sea;
> The hills whose flowers ne'er fed the bee,
> The shore no ship has ever seen,
> Still beaten by the billows green,
> Whose murmur comes unceasingly
> Unto the place for which I cry . . .
>   Yet tottering as I am and weak,
> Still have I left a little breath
> To seek within the jaws of death
> An entrance to that happy place,
> To seek the unforgotten face
> Once seen, once kissed, once reft from me
> Anigh the murmuring of the sea.

WILLIAM MORRIS

The long quest for a happier dream-land in *The
Earthly Paradise* and the later romances, the quest for
a dream-mistress in *Love is Enough* are both fore-
shadowed here; just as the stoic answer Morris was
to make to his own horror of death and division in
Sigurd the Volsung is anticipated here too in the song of
Orpheus:

> Ah once again, ah once again
>   The black prow plunges through the sea,
> Nor yet shall all your toil be vain,
>   Nor ye forgot, O Minyae.

The Earthly Paradise of 1870 remains Morris's best-
known work. Certainly some of the tales in its series
of alternate Greek and medieval legends establish him
as the greatest master of long narrative in modern
English poetry. But perhaps what lovers of Morris
remember most of all, is the wistful beauty of its
intervening lyrics, and of the scattered verses in the
stories themselves, that picture the passing of the
seasons, and of human life, sadder than the seasons in
that it never comes again. That is still the thought
that haunts the poet in the mid fire and flush of May:

For then methought the Lord of Love went by
To take possession of his flowery throne,
Ringed round with maids and youths, and minstrelsy;
A little while I sighed to find him gone,
A little while the dawning was alone,

And the light gathered; then I held my breath,
And shuddered at the sight of Eld and Death.

Alas! Love passed me in the twilight dim,
His music hushed the wakening ousel's song;
But on these twain shone out the golden sun,
And o'er their heads the brown bird's tune was strong,
As shivering 'twixt the trees they stole along;
None noted aught their noiseless passing by,
The world had quite forgotten it must die.

Morris himself could not forget. Yet it was really
love's passing that tore him even more. I know no
biographical basis to support it, but Morris's poetry
always gives me the impression of an intense capacity
for feeling starved by circumstance; as if, even, some
of the hectic activity of his life might have been partly
goaded on by a need to escape from the memory of
that.

Love while ye may; if twain grow into one,
'Tis for a little while; the time goes by,
No hatred 'twixt the pair of friends doth lie,
No troubles break their hearts—and yet, and yet—
How could it be? We strove not to forget,
Rather in vain to that old time we clung,
Its hopes and wishes round our hearts we hung,
We played old parts, we used old names—in vain,
We go our ways and twain once more are twain;
Let pass, at latest when we come to die,
Thus shall the fashion of the world go by.

As we read that bitter crowning line, there may flash

across the memory, whether it be coincidence or influence, the yet bitterer words of Wyatt centuries
before:

> It was no dream; for I lay broad awaking;
>   But all is turned now, through my gentleness,
> Into a strange fashion of forsaking;
>   And I have leave to go of her goodness.

What remedy, what help for "the idle singer of an
empty day"? The answer makes its first appearance
in *The Earthly Paradise* itself; in one of its stories, *The
Lovers of Gudrun*, which is based on the *Laxdaela Saga*,
Morris enters into his Icelandic kingdom and begins
that transition from romance to epic which was to end
in *Sigurd the Volsung*. The change of atmosphere to this
bleak northern world from the flower-like beauty of
his earlier laments is as startling as the contrast felt in
Andrew Lang's Sonnet on the *Odyssey*, between "the
songs of modern speech" and the fresh wind that
blows shouting across Homeric seas. Here too is
Love as of old; but he wields sterner arrows and a
bitterer bow among this northern race —

> Who for the rest while yet they dwelt on earth
> Wearied no God with prayers for more of mirth
> Than dying men have; nor were ill-content
> Because no God beside their sorrow went
> Turning to flowery sward the rock-strewn way,
> Weakness to strength, or darkness into day.

Two years after *The Earthly Paradise*, in 1872, appeared *Love is Enough*, an experiment in the form of a Morality Play, but delicately elaborated with framework within framework, action within action, metre within metre. There is surprisingly little hidden treasure in English Literature, for Time is a master-critic and few good things escape him; but this brief Interlude has, I think, been too much overlooked except for a few of its lyrics—

Love is enough: ho ye who seek saving,
 Go no further; come hither; there have been who
  have found it,
And these know the House of Fulfilment of Craving;
 These know the Cup with the roses around it;
 These know the World's wound and the balm that
  hath bound it:
Cry out, the World heedeth not, "Love, lead us
 home!"

O hearken the words of his voice of compassion:
 "Come, cling round about me, ye faithful who
  sicken
Of the weary unrest and the world's passing fashion!
 As the rain in mid-morning your troubles shall
  thicken,
But surely within you some Godhead doth quicken,
As ye cry to me heeding and leading you home".

But it was only an interlude. Love was not enough. Morris was growing older; and the shadow of the world's injustice darkening over him would not let him rest, busy toiler as he was, from plunging now into the muddy depths of politics as an agitating Socialist. *Sigurd the Volsung*, which tells the story of the *Volsunga Saga*, the older, finer, sterner Northern version of the legend of the *Nibelungenlied*, was finished on the eve of Morris's first political action. It may seem remote from the questions of 1876; Rossetti enraged Morris on a famous occasion by declaring that he could take no interest in a man whose brother turned into a dragon. But Ibsen's *Little Eyolf* is not made remote from the modern middle-class world that it satirizes, by the appearance in it of the Rat Wife; and those who know what was fermenting in the mind of Morris in these years, will see clearly enough what he meant by the hoard of the Elf Andvari and the curse its barren glitter brought upon the noblest and the best.

Sigurd, though its author's favourite, has never been popular. It is too long, and its metre too monotonous. *The Earthly Paradise* is also long; but its single tales are not; and it is written in three metres, not in one. Yet *Sigurd* repays its lovers; not only by the splendour of isolated passages, but by the whole impression that it leaves. Badly constructed, it has yet a unity of atmosphere not soon forgotten; not so much a philosophy of life as an attitude towards it. That is not perhaps a quality highly valued by boudoir critics who love their literature chastely divorced from real life; that under the stress of bombardments, for instance, when it was hard to remember anything, lines of *Sigurd* should echo calmingly across the memory, means nothing in their scales of value. To others it may seem a sign of power worth many twitterings. But quite apart from that there remains in this poem the terrible dramatic force of what is after all one of the great love-stories of the world—the cheated passion of Brynhild and the vengeance of Gudrun; and also a power of description in Morris (he had visited Iceland in the interval) which has hardened, indeed, but not lost its cunning, since *The Earthly Paradise.*

But forth by dale and lealand doth the son of Sigmund wend,
Till far away lies Lymdale and the folk of the forest's end;
And he rides a heath unpeopled and holds the westward way,
Till a long way off before him come up the mountains grey;
Grey, huge beyond all telling, and the host of the heaped clouds,
The black and the white together, on that rock-wall's coping crowds;
But whiles are rents athwart them, and the hot sun pierceth through,

And there glow the angry cloud-caves 'gainst the
   everlasting blue,
And the changeless snow amidst it; but down from
   that cloudy head
The scars of fires that have been, show grim and
   dusky-red,
And lower yet are the hollows striped down by the
   scanty green,
And lingering flecks of the cloud-host are tangled
   there between,
White, pillowy, lit by the sun, unchanged by the drift
   of the wind.

Morris must indeed have thought of himself as he
wrote those words of Regin the Smith:

The toil that each dawning quickens, and the task
   that is never done;
And the heart that longeth ever, nor will look to the
   deed that is won.

For as each of his own long tasks attained its end,
he felt all Gibbon's sadness at the close of the *Decline
and Fall*, and was not comforted until he was well
launched on some new venture. But with *Sigurd* his
poetic work was nearly done; *Poems by the Way* and
Chants for Socialists are less important; he turned back
more and more, like Shakespeare, to romances, but
to prose romances, as his life drew towards its close.
Yet the real world was with him to the last; he wrote
of wells at the world's end and of woods beyond it,

amid the clatter of Hammersmith milk-carts and in the intervals of tub-thumping at street-corners in Walham Green, or of printing at the Kelmscott Press. When in 1896 the end came and he was carried in a flower-hung farm-cart to his sleep in Kelmscott Churchyard, there above his bones might well have been written the old epitaph: "Here rests one that never rested before".

Morris would not have greatly cared what the critics of the future said about his books so long as there were still readers to be happy over them. With his passion for positive achievement and his hatred of unreality, he had little love for most criticism of the arts: "What's the good of making a damned fuss about it? One likes a picture because it's jolly well done and there's an end of it". He felt that a man had far better go and do as well himself, if he could, or hold his tongue, if he couldn't. He underestimated the uses of criticism (it too is an art for which there is both time and need), but less, I think, than we now exaggerate them. To-day, at all events, he has still his readers, devoted rather than numerous. He is not on the highway of literature. He wrote too much; he would have been wise to labour longer and leave his works shorter; like almost all poets, and more than most, he failed to realize what a power of con-centration poetry has, and what power it can gain from concentration—how often, in a word, "the half is more than the whole". None the less, I believe that, among our modern poets, he is "a good life". He wrote less to please his age than most Victorian writers; and so survives it more lastingly. The things he cared for, the world also will come, I believe, to care for more and more, if it is to get any better. *News from Nowhere* may be a dream; it too much ignores science and machinery; but compared with it other Utopias are nightmares. As men grow tired of their mechanical toys, and lose belief in any future life, they may come to feel the folly of making the world they inhabit so briefly into a hell of hideousness and overcrowding and overwork, when it might be a place, of death indeed and suffering and unhappy love, but also of natural beauty and health and happy labour. An England with a quarter the population and one-tenth the factories of to-day, no longer earning as "the world's workshop" the estimable privilege of maintaining so many extra million drudges in an existence they would be better without, might hereafter come to find Morris one of the wisest of his century. But independently of that his poetry will, I believe, be read and remembered as long as there exist minds romantic enough to rebel against the prosaic materialism of modern civilization, and yet too realistic to turn away from the solid, pagan earth in chase of mystic dreams. Between the fireside glitter of societies like Pope's and the sun-blinded vapours of souls like Shelley's, lies a middle sphere. In it are found reason without insensitiveness and imagination without unreality, sense without hardness and deep feeling without sentiment; in it the greatest name is Shakespeare, and far from the least is William Morris.

IX

SWINBURNE

On en rit, c'est hasard s'il n'a heurté personne;
Mais sa folie au front lui met une couronne,
A l'épaule une pourpre, et devant son chemin
La flûte et les flambeaux, comme au jeune Romain.

ALFRED DE MUSSET.

In bed in a room at Eton sits a little boy with green eyes and red hair—a vast flaming mop of it—eating his tea while a maid reads aloud to him: all of a sudden the level droning of her voice rises into a scream—the patient has just crowned her head with the jam-pot from the tea-tray, turned neatly upside down. That gesture is prophetic. For the little boy is Algernon Swinburne, and he is to leap into fame a few years hence by upsetting the domestic delicacy of the Victorians joyously and maliciously on their own heads. The episode is indeed typical of the future poet in another way as well; emptying jam-pots on maid-servants' heads is a distinctly youthful form of humour —it is even a little cruel; and the distinctive thing about Swinburne, both as a person and as a poet, is that he never grew up. He remained to the end of his seventy-two years exuberantly young. The touch of cruelty too was there. Certainly he changed little after leaving Oxford; much in him never grew beyond Eton; he kept always a good deal of the aristocratic school-boy, childish even in his handwriting to the last.

For like several other great rebels (he noted it him-self), like Landor and Mirabeau, like Byron and Shelley, the son of Admiral Swinburne and Lady Ashburnham was an aristocrat. The Swinburnes had lived and fought on the Northumbrian Border since Edward II's day; the Ashburnhams were "the ancientest family which can be instructed to have been of good account in England before the Conquest", and Bertram de Eshburnham, Sheriff of Sussex, had lost his head for holding Dover Castle against William the Norman. Eton was always remembered by the poet with affection; Oxford was not. His University career he himself described as "a total and scandalous failure"; though there he met two of the main influences in his life, Benjamin Jowett, soon to be Master of Balliol, and Dante Gabriel Rossetti, who came at this time to paint the Union. At all events the Swinburne who had gone up to Oxford in 1856 with ideas of entering the Church, went down to London in 1860 with very different intentions. His first volume of two verse plays fell flat; but in 1865 appeared *Atalanta in Calydon*, which may be described as an attack on religion in the form of a Greek tragedy and in the language of the Old Testament. It was audaciously outspoken; Christina Rossetti, who admired her brother's wild young friend, kept a piece of paper pasted over one particularly impious line—"the supreme evil, God"— in her copy of the play; but to the eyes of the public at large, only half opened as yet to what had arisen in their midst, the impiety was masked by the poetry

—poetry with such a rush and lilt about it as had never been heard in English verse before.

> For winter's rains and ruins are over,
>   And all the season of snows and sins;
> The days dividing lover and lover,
>   The light that loses, the night that wins;
> And time remembered is grief forgotten,
> And frosts are slain and flowers begotten,
> And in green underwood and cover
>   Blossom by blossom the spring begins.
>
> The full streams feed on flower of rushes,
>   Ripe grasses trammel a travelling foot,
> The faint fresh flame of the young year flushes
>   From leaf to flower and flower to fruit;
> And fruit and leaf are as gold and fire,
> And the oat is heard above the lyre,
> And the hoofèd heel of a satyr crushes
>   The chestnut-husk at the chestnut-root.

The public had not long to wait, however, before its eyes were opened very wide indeed. In the next year, 1866 (exactly half a century after that famous paroxysm of morality in which the British public hounded Byron for ever from our shores), was published a volume called *Poems and Ballads*; and at one stroke Swinburne, whose *Atalanta* had been merely a pleasant success, found himself an object of shrieking horror, an outcast, an abomination. Imagine the effect, in an England, whose heir-apparent in his boyhood had been forbidden even the novels of Scott, and whose womenfolk, when caught with *Jane Eyre*, had slipped the guilty volume under the sofa-cushions, of opening a book and reading—

> What ailed us, O gods, to desert you
> For creeds that refuse and restrain?
> Come down and redeem us from virtue,
> Our Lady of Pain.

Or again, with the same mixture of youthful insolence and aged disillusion—

> Time turns the old things to derision
> And our loves into corpses or wives,
> And marriage and death and division
> Make barren our lives.

As Rossetti said, "poeta nascitur, non fit for publication". To-day, indeed, such writing seems curiously naïve, almost innocent; we enjoy the lilt of it and smile at the fanfaronade; but it was no smiling matter in 1866. One publisher refused the book. A second apprehensively dropped it, at the last minute, like a hot coal. The third was menaced with prosecution. The reviewers, John Morley among them, lifted up their voices and howled in chorus. Righteous fury even led the owner of a picture by Legros with a cat in it to have the cat painted out, because the creature had been praised by Swinburne at the exhibition. On the other hand no less frenzied

admirers went down on their knees in drawing-rooms
and adored the poet, while bands of undergraduates
linked arm in arm startled the staid streets of University towns with the chanting of those unspeakable
stanzas. Swinburne had made his name with a vengeance. He had been quite well aware what he was
doing: "I have added", he had written to a friend
with impish glee, "yet four more jets of boiling and
gushing infamy to the perennial and poisonous foun-
tain of *Dolores*". What zest! He was still very youthful,
this young man of twenty-eight. But his elders were
beginning to wonder if he were indeed old enough to
look after himself; for in the Bohemia of London
Swinburne was fast racketing away his health. In
1862 he had met at the house of some friends of
Ruskin's a young woman called Jane Faulkner; she
was amused by this strange, fragile little poet with his
red aureole of hair and his birdlike, fluttering ways;
she brought him roses; she played to him; perhaps
she played a little with him. One day he suddenly
proposed to her; and, partly perhaps out of sheer
astonished nervousness, she broke into a fit of laughter.
The ignominious agony of that moment and the
bitter resentment that followed it, have left their mark
on Swinburne's poetry.

> Let us go hence, my songs; she will not hear.
> Let us go hence together without fear;

Keep silence now, for singing-time is over,
And over all old things and all things dear.
She loves not you nor me as all we love her.
Yea, though we sang as angels in her ear,
      She would not hear.

And again:

In the change of years, in the coil of things,
   In the clamour and rumour of life to be,
We, drinking love at the furthest springs,
   Covered with love as a covering tree,
We had grown as gods, as the gods above,
Filled from the heart to the lips with love,
Held fast in his hands, clothed warm with his wings,
   O love, my love, had you loved but me! . . .

You have chosen and clung to the chance they sent you,
   Life sweet as a perfume and pure as prayer.
But will it not one day in heaven repent you?
   Will they solace you wholly, the days that were?
Will you lift up your eyes between sadness and bliss,
Meet mine, and see where the great love is,
And tremble and turn and be changed? Content you;
   The gate is strait; I shall not be there. . . .

I shall never be friends again with roses;
   I shall loathe sweet tunes, where a note grown strong
Relents and recoils, and climbs and closes,
   As a wave of the sea turned back by song.
There are sounds where the soul's delight takes fire,
Face to face with its own desire;
A delight that rebels, a desire that reposes;
   I shall hate sweet music my whole life long.

What mark the incident left on Swinburne's life as well, it is harder to say; perhaps a deep one. He never seems to have thought again of marriage; and it is possible that the abnormality of temperament which left barren and embittered all his emotional life, so that for him love's pleasure became tangled with a morbid desire for pain, was branded more deeply and irremovably upon him by this disappointment.

At all events both his life and his poetry became more perverse after it; until in 1867 Jowett and other friends met to discuss "what could be done *with* and *for* Algernon". The influence of Mazzini, the exiled Italian patriot whom the poet had worshipped since boyhood, was invoked; and he successfully persuaded Swinburne that there must be "no more of this love-frenzy", that he must abandon passionate poetry for political poetry, the praise of Venus for that of Italian Unity. *Songs before Sunrise* appeared in consequence, in 1871. There the poet's morals are doubtless much improved; his poetry, I think, is not; but on that point opinions differ. In any case the eternal child in him remained as incompetent as ever to cope with the world; and in 1879, when the damage to his health had become really alarming, he was carried off by one Watts-Dunton, a literary solicitor, to Putney, where he was kept in cotton-wool for the remaining thirty years of his life, till he was laid to rest at Bon-

church, in 1909. It was an ironic ending to the story
—the "demoniac youth", as Ruskin called him,
who had so fluttered the dove-cotes of the Victorians,
turned at last into a healthy, methodical little old
gentleman of clockwork habits, his only dissipation
a morning walk over Wimbledon Common and his
only excitement (apart from literary quarrels of a
quite frenzied ferocity) the dances of ecstasy he used
to perform round every perambulator encountered
on the way. For Mr Watts-Dunton, though kind, was
strict; and Swinburne was not even allowed to use
improper language at table except in French, because
of the servants. The tiger-cat was tamed, the rebel
subdued; once more Victorianism had won. Rossetti
it had driven mad; Swinburne it simply swallowed
alive. The author of *Dolores* grew to be shocked by
Shakespeare's *Venus and Adonis*; the voice that had
hymned the Liberation of Italy and the fall of the
Second Empire turned in the end to execrate the
monstrous pretensions to freedom of Ireland and the
Transvaal Republic. Yet, through all these changes,
he remained the schoolboy still, in his enthusiasms
and his violences, his hatreds and his hero-worship.
"Isn't he the damnedest simulacrum?" exclaimed
Walt Whitman, when Swinburne suddenly passed
from praising to rending *Leaves of Grass*. The same
boyish irresponsibility runs through all the anecdotes

of his life; he is always the same highly-strung, uncontrolled *enfant terrible*, now dining off a roast monkey at Havre or doing a war-dance on the top-hats in the hall of a London club in his fury at failing to find his own (which, as it happened, he had not brought with him); now reading aloud his most improper poems at a house-party to the Archbishop of York, or slapping Meredith's face, or writing to Emerson to "inform" him that he was "a hoary-headed and toothless baboon".

So with his poetry—its essential faults and excellences are alike those of youth. In some degree we may apply to all of it his own words on *Poems and Ballads I.* "The youngest were born of boy's pastime, The eldest are young." His work has indeed the typical defects of youth—want of experience and judgment, of proportion and restraint. It strives and cries; at times it screeches. Having few ideas, it grows monotonous; having little knowledge of the heart, it lacks compassion. Brilliant and hard, it reflects the light of life with a glare like polished brass; with all its music, it is often brass to the ear; it is sometimes, in its taste, brass also to the tongue. There is about Swinburne a touch of the musical infant-prodigy. This immaturity did not escape his elder contemporaries. Tennyson spoke contemptuously of "Master Swinburne", Matthew Arnold dubbed him "a pseudo-Shelley"; Browning described his work as "a fuzz of words" and Carlyle (it is said) as "the miaulings of a delirious cat". But they were blind if they saw no more in it than that; for the splendour of youth is also there—its fire, its generosity, its passionate high spirits, its racing pulses, its headlong speed—

> Albeit I die indeed
> And hide myself and sleep and no man heed,
> Of me the high God hath not all his will.
> Blossom of branches, and on each high hill
> Clear air and wind, and under in clamorous vales
> Fierce noises of the fiery nightingales,
> Buds burning in the sudden spring like fire,
> The wan washed sand and the waves' vain desire,
> Sails seen like blown white flowers at sea, and words
> That bring tears swiftest, and long notes of birds
> Violently singing till the whole world sings—
> I Sappho shall be one with all these things,
> With all high things for ever. . . .
> Yea, they shall say, earth's womb has borne in vain
> New things, and never this best thing again;
> Borne days and men, borne fruits and wars and wine,
> Seasons and songs, but no song more like mine.

Still, as time passes, the defects of youthfulness in his poetry seem to me to grow at the expense of the virtues; he wrote best, I feel, when he was really young. The heart of him is in *Atalanta* and *Poems and Ballads*; after thirty, his bloom begins to fade. Others think otherwise; he himself preferred the chants of Liberty in *Songs before Sunrise*. But there are subjects that come more kindly to youthful poets than world-politics—after all, world-politics do ask some knowledge of the world. The inspiration of Catullus and Chatterton, of Keats and Alfred de Musset lies elsewhere—in their passionate sense of love and beauty, of death and rebellion against death. This joining of youth and death may seem a paradox; yet it is perfectly natural and inevitable that youth, in its very fullness of joy and life, should resent with wild intensity the sorrow and mortality it sees darkening the horizons of its bright new world. This may be a transient mood; yet it is an eternally recurrent one, and from it some of the world's most immortal poetry has sprung. To-day we may not feel very lyrical about the French Republic; what happened to Italian Liberty everyone knows; but human suffering is always with us—

For who shall change with prayers or thanksgivings
The mystery of the cruelty of things?

Age accepts; but youth cries out in anger, or broods in bitterness.

Why hath he made us? What had all we done
That we should live and loathe the sterile sun,
And with the moon wax paler as she wanes,
And pulse by pulse feel time grow through our veins?

The protest may be idle; but at least the utterance of
it kindled Swinburne in *Atalanta* to an eloquence that
even he was never to surpass—

Thou hast sent us sleep, and stricken sleep with
    dreams,
  Saying, Joy is not, but love of joy shall be;
Thou hast made sweet springs for all the pleasant
    streams,
  In the end thou hast made them bitter with the sea.
Thou hast fed one rose with dust of many men;
  Thou hast marred one face with fire of many tears;
Thou hast taken love, and given us sorrow again;
  With pain thou hast filled us full to the eyes and ears.
Therefore because thou art strong, our father, and we
  Feeble; and thou art against us, and thine hand
Constrains us in the shallows of the sea
  And breaks us at the limits of the land . . .
Because thou art over all who are over us;
  Because thy name is life, and our name death;
Because thou art cruel and men are piteous,
  And our hands labour and thine hand scattereth;
Lo, with hearts rent and knees made tremulous,
  Lo, with ephemeral lips and casual breath,
  At least we witness of thee ere we die
That these things are not otherwise, but thus.

In *Poems and Ballads I*, the poet turns his rebellious
anger less against the laws of God than against the
laws of men, as the outraged Victorians were quick to
realize; towards death and destiny his mood is more
resigned. Yet it is still the resignation not of middle-

age which learns to ignore death, but of youth which half falls in love with it, as at moments Keats had done. So Swinburne too grows dreamily fascinated by the dreamless slumber of the dead:

In deep wet ways by grey old gardens
Fed with sharp spring the sweet fruit hardens;
    They know not what fruits wane or grow;
Red summer burns to the utmost ember;
They know not, neither can remember
    The old years and flowers they used to know. . . .

Wind wherein stars and seas are shaken
Shall shake them, and they shall not waken;
    None that has lain down shall arise;
The stones are sealed across their places;
One shadow is shed on all their faces,
    One blindness cast on all their eyes.

This passion indeed linked itself in him with that deep-rooted instinct which made him crave to suffer at the hands of what he loved. He had written in *Atalanta* of a devoted son who dies at his own mother's hand, in *Chastelard* of a Queen's lover who forces her to send him to the block; now the Goddess of Death herself became for him, as it were, a mysterious mistress whose cold caress brings peace.

Pale, beyond porch and portal,
    Crowned with calm leaves, she stands
Who gathers all things mortal
    With cold immortal hands;

Her languid lips are sweeter
Than Love's, who fears to greet her,
To men that mix and meet her
    From many times and lands.

She waits for each and other,
    She waits for all men born;
Forgets the earth her mother,
    The life of fruits and corn;
And spring and seed and swallow
Take wing for her and follow
Where summer song rings hollow
    And flowers are put to scorn.

Morbid? Yes: but what music! That music Swinburne had always at command. Justice is not always
done to this amazing gift of his. This is partly because
he abused it by singing on and on with nothing
new to say; for certainly there are long poems of his
to which I can imagine an enemy applying his own
description of the Dunwich coast:

Miles on miles on miles of desolation,
Leagues on leagues on leagues without a change.

But partly, too, he has been defeated by his own
success and lost in his own brilliance; fatal to imitate,
impossible to eclipse, he lacks followers to defend him.
For fatal to imitate he certainly remains; as H. D.
Traill has gaily put it—

They strut like jays in my lendings,
  They chatter and screech; I sing.
They mimic my phrases and endings
  And rum Old Testament ring.
But the lyrical cry isn't in it
And the high gods spot in a minute
  That it isn't the genuine thing.

Unfortunately, as years passed, living subjects came more and more to fail him. He grew abstract and vague; he never ripened. He tried to make literature out of literature, a form of in-breeding almost always fatal and sterile. The nightingale in him died of too much midnight oil. His plays and his narrative poems lack knowledge of human nature; his characters talk like archangels, but they do not live or feel or act like men and women. Nor could he paint Nature like Tennyson; he is a poet not of the eye but of the ear, and his work is almost colour-blind. His images are all white fire and foam and fury; even his nightingales are "fierce", even his buds "burn".

And yet even in the later volumes, when the flame of his eloquence can find something real to feed it, the old splendour suddenly flares heaven-high again.

On Aikenshaw the sun shinks braw,
  The burn rins blythe and fain;
There's nought wi'me I wadna gie
  To look thereon again.

On Keilder-side the wind blaws wide;
  There sounds nae hunting-horn
That rings sae sweet as the winds that beat
  Round banks where Tyne is born.

The Wansbeck sings with all her springs,
  The bents and braes give ear;
But the wood that rings wi'the sang she sings
  I may not see nor hear;
For far and far thae blithe burns are,
  And strange is a' thing near.

Some of these imitations of the Border Ballads, where he was forced to be hard instead of hazy, direct instead of roundabout, remain unforgettable; some of his songs of Liberty can wake echoes still. There too he was vague; the nineteenth century had yet to learn how little political freedom matters, so long as economic slavery remains. Perhaps the twentieth century is making the opposite mistake. The Termite-state is a poor Eldorado. Certainly, in this age when dictators are all the fashion and perorate complacently about "the putrid corpse of Liberty", there are lines in Swinburne's *Mater Triumphalis*, that ring out like a trumpet-blast above her tomb:

We have known thee and have not known thee; stood
    beside thee,
  Felt thy lips breathe, set foot where thy feet trod,
Loved and renounced and worshipped and denied thee,
  As if thou wert but as another God. . . .

SWINBURNE

Death is subdued to thee, and Hell's bands broken;
  Where thou art only is Heaven; who hears not thee,
Time shall not hear him; when men's names are
    spoken,
  A nameless sign of death shall his name be. . . .

Thou sayest "Well done", and all a century kindles;
  Again thou sayest "Depart from sight of me",
And all the light of face of all men dwindles,
  And the age is as the broken glass of thee.

Swinburne stands beside Byron as the poet of eloquence, and of Liberty. There is indeed a distance between them—the distance between Putney and Missolonghi. Byron acted; Swinburne did not. And accordingly Byron's poetry grew better with age; Swinburne's worse. But youthful as Swinburne's poetry essentially is, I believe that a little of the best of it, generations hence, will remain, still full of youth.

X

HARDY

"On est tout étonné et ravi, car on s'attendait de voir un auteur, et on trouve un homme."

PASCAL.

It is not generally realized that it was Plato who first conceived the cinema. (How annoyed he would have been, could he but have known it!) Turn to one of his most famous passages, and there it is: mankind, he says in the *Republic*, are like dwellers in a cave who watch passing before them a stream of shadow-shapes, thrown by a light behind them on a wall in front. That is all we know of reality—shadows, only shadows. The philosopher alone, Plato continues, can grope his way out of the cavern into the light of day and see things as they really are. We may indeed feel that most philosophers, including Plato himself, have only exchanged ordinary shadows for new ones of their own, more shadowy still. However it is a poet that here concerns us, a poet that Plato would have banished more sternly even than most of them from his Utopia—Thomas Hardy; and I have only quoted Plato's image of shadow and reality to illustrate the essential difference I feel between Hardy and the generality of poets. For the light that most of them throw before us is that of a magic lantern, with shapes of lovely illusion and a radiance no earthly sun can throw. When we shut their volumes, it is with a start that we come back to the world of everyday, as if we were waking from a dream; just as a cinema audience, stealthily wiping the last moisture from the corners of its eyes, streams out of its shadow-world of ravishing and ravished heroines into that grey daylight where trains are caught and kettles boil for tea. This is natural enough. Much poetry is merely daydreaming made immortal by the magic power of words; and mediaeval poets regularly pretended to have dreamed their poems—works, very often, in which the poet falls asleep at the beginning, and the reader in the middle. But with Hardy it is different; it is not a dream that he seems to bring before us, but a vision; not some vista remote from the reality we live in, but a vision of that reality more vivid than our own. He does not come to create illusion, but to destroy it; indeed he makes us realize how much illusion we have to cling to in our daily life in order to go on living it at all. The truth of his poetry is ruthless: its only comfort lies in the tenderness of its sensitive imagination and the splendour of its quiet sincerity. There are moments when it makes other poetry seem frivolous. Through the pages of Hardy, I feel, one does not so much read as live.

What made Hardy so truthful? Mainly, I suppose, that he was born so. Explanations of such things explain little, at best. But we can see, I think, how circumstances helped. The child who opened his eyes in the year 1840 in a master-mason's home near Dorchester, was brought from the first into contact with a ruder side of life than most of our poets. His home was not a poor one; but it was in touch with the earth of Wessex and the peasantry that tilled it. Even childhood was taken seriously by this little boy who was in later life to remember how he sat one day in the garden among the ferns, wishing he need never become any older or more grown-up. One feels, indeed, that like the child of Jude the Obscure, Hardy himself was born grown-up; that, if Swinburne was always young, Hardy never was. From school he passed to an architect's office in Dorchester; and thence, appropriately enough, to restoring old churches up and down in Wessex. That too must have helped to mould him.

For the architect is of all artists the least able to indulge in airy dreams. Bricks and mortar, strains and stresses, the relentless drag of the earth and the buffets of the stormy sky are no playthings. A Shelley may build his palaces in the clouds and launch his paper boats down the stream of Time; an earthly architect, who listens like Ibsen's Master Builder to "harps in the air", will soon break other men's necks as well as his own.

Scraps of *Far from the Madding Crowd* Hardy scribbled at odd moments out of doors on large leaves, chips of wood, pieces of stone; that might well have been true, one feels, of all his writing, so close seems its touch, from its first moment of conception, with real and concrete things. Here is never a stain nor smell of midnight oil.

Further, of all the arts, no other is so desperately at war as the architect's with Time. The written word can be reprinted for ever; the notes of the musician spring as fresh from the string to-day as the first time they were played; painter and sculptor work in material almost imperishable. But for the architect, before the tiles are on his roof, Time's noiseless feet are already hollowing his stairs, Time's fingers tearing at his masonry with the lash of wind and rain. Now two of the fundamental things in Hardy are his stern sense of Reality and his saddened sense of Time. Though this sense of transience, it must be added, was clearly rooted in Hardy's nature from the first: even as a child he used to sit and watch the last glow of sunset on the red staircase wall at home, reciting to himself Dr Watts's "And now another day is gone". Equally characteristic is the entry in his Journal at the close of 1865: "To insects the twelvemonth has been an epoch, to leaves a life, to tweeting birds a generation, to man a year".

From architecture he turned to fiction. With that he won his fame. For a quarter of a century he wrote it, until in 1895 the British Public had another of its spasms of outraged morality over *Jude the Obscure*. The episode recalls the equally ridiculous uproar over Swinburne's *Poems and Ballads* thirty years before; the two authors were indeed regarded by the righteous as confederates in iniquity: "Swinburne planteth", said a Scottish journal, "Hardy watereth, and Satan giveth the increase". Howled down as a novelist, Hardy turned back to poetry; he had always loved verse better than prose; now for the first time he began to publish it.

But even on his poetry the novelist in him, as well as the architect, has left his mark. Few English poets have written good novels, except Meredith; few, one imagines, except Chaucer and Shakespeare, could have. Writers like Milton or Gray or Wordsworth or Tennyson tend to be too self-centred. For the novelist must understand others; and it is this power of subtle sympathy that makes so poignant much of Hardy's verse.

Such, then, is the personality behind it—an architect who has struggled with solid earth and masonry, a novelist who has lived and suffered in hearts outside his own; and, underneath, a Wessex countryman seeing life with the mingled grimness and tenderness, irony and pity of those who see life at its hardest. There lies the contrast between him and Meredith; who looked on the world less steadily, and less compassionately also. There was less of the woman in him than in Hardy; and he was the smaller man in consequence. In Meredith the head outgrew the heart; he tended to prefer cleverness to wisdom, brilliance to truth.

But how does this truthfulness show itself in Hardy's work? Partly in his sincerity, the sense he gives of never having written a line he did not feel; but still more in his intellectual honesty. With most people there is an incorrigible tendency to believe what they want to believe, because it would be so pleasant if only it were true. The wish with them is father to the thought; and the thought is generally a bastard and deceptive thought in consequence. There are poets like Tennyson who think of Beauty before Truth; they tend to produce poetry that is perfect rather than great: and there are poets like Hardy who have a feeling for Truth even before Beauty; these tend to produce poetry that is great rather than perfect.

> Between us now and here
> Two thrown together . . .
> Let there be truth at last
> Even if despair.

Those last two lines might make the motto of all Hardy's work.

As Reuben the Tranter says: "Well, now, that coarseness that's so upsetting to Ann's feelings, is to

my mind a recommendation; for it do always prove
a story to be true. And for the same reason, I like a
story with a bad moral. My sonnies, all true stories
have a coarseness or a bad moral, depend on't. If the
story-tellers could have got decency and good morals
from stories, who'd ha' troubled to invent parables?"
The logic is not flawless; Reuben is not Hardy; but
a family likeness is there—the same hatred of cant.
"Write a list", runs an entry in Hardy's Journal for
1883, "of things which everybody thinks and nobody
says; and a list of things that everybody says and nobody thinks." If a particular instance of this passion
for truth is needed, we may contrast his view of
Nature with Wordsworth's. The two poets have much
in common. Both turned back from the sophistication
of great cities to the simplicity and sincerity of the
countryside—

Love had *they* found in huts where poor men lie.

But for Wordsworth Nature could do no wrong: for
Hardy all her beauty could not hide her witless
cruelty. In a vernal wood Wordsworth found more
lessons of moral good and evil than in all the sages put
together; there is a certain truth in that, no doubt, but
not truth enough—less than in Hardy's vision of the
death-struggle for a place in the sun that rages there
between tree and tree, between plant and parasite,

189

none the less grimly because it is too silent for us to hear, too slow for us to see. Nature is radiantly beautiful—let us feast our eyes; but she is also a blind fiend—let us face that too. In the twentieth century the human herd tends more to turn its heads rather than its tails to the storm of life; so that Wordsworth's caressing hand now rubs us the wrong way. If it is a question of "goodness", give us men with all their faults, not trees.

> Touches from ash, O wych,
>   Sting you like scorn!
> You, too, brave hollies twitch
>   Sidelong from thorn.
> Even the rank poplars bear
> Lothly a rival's air,
> Cankering in black despair
>   If overborne.
>
> Since, then, no grace I find
>   Taught me of trees,
> Turn I back to my kind,
>   Worthy as these.
> There at least smiles abound,
> There discourse trills around,
> There, now and then, are found
>   Life-loyalties.

"Funny man, Browning!"—said Hardy once (so a friend has told me), "all that optimism! He must have put it in to please the public. He *can't* have

believed it." This is not a judgment to be taken too
seriously; but it is characteristic, I think.

This lifelong refusal to shut his eyes to the un-
welcome or hide his head in the sand makes much of
Hardy's writing inevitably sad. Existence trailed for
him no clouds of glory.

> "I do not promise overmuch,
>   Child, overmuch.
> Just neutral-tinted haps and such,"
>   You said to minds like mine.

But it is not sad poetry that is depressing; it is bad
poetry. Truth about life calmly faced kills no one not
sick already. The snake that was once found curled
harmlessly asleep on the little Hardy's chest in childhood, might serve for a symbol of that. And he had
his own consolations, lasting ones, in a sense of life's
tragic beauty, and also of its tragic irony. Because he
was haunted by Time and transience, because he
never saw the commonest thing without a vision of
what it once had been or what it one day would be,
in return even the commonest things were lit for him
with a gleam of tragic poetry. He saw things as in-
stinctively in three tenses as in three dimensions. In
this way he widened the domain of poetry till it became for him as wide as life itself, a life intensely sad
and yet intensely real. The comfort that religion
failed to give, he found and thought that others might

find, not necessarily in writing poetry about this world, but in seeing this world poetically, as anyone with an imagination can. Philosophy, as I have said elsewhere, demands that we take her dreams for truth; poetry, more wisely, offers her dreams as dreams alone. And Hardy found her in the simplest things—a milestone by a rabbit-burrow, or an old log upon the fire, raindrops on a door-step, or green tiles high up a roof; no subject was too minute for that vast vision of his which had yet in *The Dynasts* seen Napoleon's Grande Armée as a creeping caterpillar and had versified even the curving space of Einstein in the last volume of his old age. Hardy did not simply make poetry out of life; he made life into poetry.

Hence yet another source of his truthfulness; he never needed to employ the fantastic passions, the remotely strained psychology of more romantic writers. He deliberately took for his subjects the commonest and most natural feelings; but by an unfamiliar side, and with that insight which only sensitiveness and sympathy can possess. This sympathy is important; for, as I have said, if truthfulness is one main feature of Hardy's work, its compassion is another. Without that, the bitter truth in his pages might seem too bitter, the irony too sardonic; but that pity which he found so wanting in the Universe, crowns his own work with perfect things like *Tess's Lament*:

> I would that folk forgot me quite,
>   Forgot me quite!
> I would that I could shrink from sight,
>   And no more see the sun.
> Would it were time to say farewell,
> To claim my nook, to need my knell,
> Time for them all to stand and tell
>   Of my day's work as done. . . .

> It wears me out to think of it,
>   To think of it;
> I cannot bear my fate as writ,
>   I'd have my life unbe;
> Would turn my memory to a blot,
> Make every relic of me rot,
> My doings be as they were not,
>   And gone all trace of me!

One day Anatole France, being baited by an American Professor as to the ultimate essence of literary genius, answered—"Pity". It was the exclamation of a moment, lightly thrown off in repartee. But, however inadequate, it is less wild than at first might seem: pity—nobility—personality—those three, as Anatole France explained, do indeed go together; not always, but often. There are modern critics who harp without ceasing on the theme that the writer must efface his personality; in their own case such abstinence may be easy; it may even be well-advised:

but in the supreme authors of the world their personality is an ineffaceable and essential part of their work. It need not be obtruded; as a rule, it is better not obtruded; but between every two lines of the greatest it is there—the footprint of the lion. Even in Stendhal it is present, even in Flaubert, behind all their impassivity. And without it, all the brains in Christendom are profitless. Which is one reason why poets are born, not made; since personality is not to be taught. It rings clear in all that Hardy wrote; and a dominant note in it is this sense of compassion. Throughout his lyrics, as through *The Dynasts*, the Spirits of the Pities and the Spirits Ironic sing alternately; but in both the Pities have the last word. He never forgave the world the red streak of cruelty that runs through all its beauty: and the divine he found, not in Heaven, but in the cage of the blinded bird that sings on still with unembittered gaiety though man with a red-hot needle has burnt out both its eyes.

Hardy's own eyes were too clear for him to sing without a note of bitterness; but sing he also could. Of all the critical imbecilities bandied about at the present day, none is sillier than the notion that Hardy is always harsh. If *Tess's Lament* be harsh, what is music? Hardy when he chose could be as liquid as Tennyson, as elaborate as Swinburne, with a simple brevity that Swinburne lacked—

Upon a poet's page I wrote
Of old two letters of her name;
Part seemed she of the effulgent thought
Whence that high singer's rapture came.
When now I turn the leaf, the same
Immortal light illumes the lay,
But from the letters of her name
The radiance has waned away.

This poet who is talked of as a sort of unshaven, guttural rustic of genius, really delighted in the elaborate delicacy of triolets like *At a Hasty Wedding*—

If hours be years, the twain are blest,
For now they solace swift desire
By bonds of every bond the best,
If hours be years. The twain are blest,
Do eastern stars slope never west,
Nor pallid ashes follow fire:
If hours be years, the twain are blest,
For now they solace swift desire;

or would set himself such difficulties as this piece of octuple masculine and, more arduous still, octuple feminine rhymes—

Never a careworn wife but shows,
    If a joy suffuse her,
Something beautiful to those
    Patient to peruse her,
Some one charm the world unknows,
    Precious to a muser
Haply what, ere years were foes,
    Moved her mate to choose her.

> But, be it a hint of rose
>   That an instant hues her,
> Or some early light or pose
>   Wherewith thought renews her—
> Seen by him at full, ere woes
>   Practised to abuse her—
> Sparely comes it, swiftly goes,
>   Time again subdues her.

But the excellence of Hardy's eloquence does not lie simply in this power of executing technical *tours de force* so naturally that they are not even noticed: it lies in the purity and sincerity, as of a perfect voice speaking quietly, that echoes through his moods of gentle, hopeless irony, as in these lines on a dead mistress—

> I need not go
> Through sleet and snow
> To where I know
> She waits for me;
> She will wait me there
> Till I find it fair,
> And have time to spare
> From company . . .
> What—not upbraid me
> That I delayed me,
> Nor ask what stayed me
> So long? Ah no!—
> New cares may claim me,
> New loves inflame me,
> She will not blame me,
> But suffer it so.

If he is at other times rough, the roughness is deliberate; for he held that Art should hide her artifice. But I doubt if any English poet has more studied the craft of verse, or invented more new metrical forms and variations. The roughness of *The Dynasts* is indeed, I think, at times excessive; though even there a certain gnarled grandeur suits the vastness of Hardy's theme. I know no work which combines such impressiveness as a whole with such rudeness in detail. But you do not polish the Pyramids, or manicure the Sphinx.

> Ha, ha, that's good! Thou'lt pray to It:—
> But where do Its Companions sit?
> Yea, where abides the heart of It?
>
> Is it where sky-fires flame and flit,
> Or solar craters spew and spit,
> Or ultra-stellar night-webs knit?
>
> What is Its shape? Man's counterfeit?
> That turns in some far sphere unlit
> The Wheel which drives the Infinite?

With Hardy an epoch ended; he outlived the passing of Queen Victoria, and the War which left the spirit of her age buried for ever beneath the mountains of its dead. He had been already a boy of ten when Wordsworth died; he had seen Victorianism growl even at Tennyson, its chosen Laureate, and ignore complacently the saturnine irony of Arnold, and bait Rossetti, and howl at Swinburne; he had felt its teeth himself. Tess of the d'Urbervilles had been called a harlot; *Jude the Obscure* enjoyed the consecration of being burnt by a bishop, who wrote proudly to the papers to proclaim his exploit, and privately to Smith's Library to suppress the book. But at least Hardy lived to see justice done.

I have tried to give a certain unity to the series of poets we have dealt with by making their background the decline and fall of the Victorian Age. It is a strange age to look back on, in its mixture of baseness and greatness. The storm of loathing and derision hurled at it by the generation which grew up in time for the First World War, was far too undiscriminating; but not unjustified. It was no ordinary reaction of one age against its predecessor. There is only one parallel to its violence and bitterness—the reaction that followed the Age of the Puritans. The true forerunner of Lytton Strachey's *Eminent Victorians* is Samuel Butler's *Hudibras*. In either case the reason is the same—the revulsion of the healthy human instincts for freedom and honesty against tyranny and cant. The great Victorians were the first to rebel; perhaps being rebels helped to make them great—knight-errants need dragons; at all events it is not easy for us to defend their own age against them. The social atmosphere which

the English middle class created in their century of
supremacy is nauseous to breathe to-day. On the
other hand, we who in our own time have done more
to defile and befoul the face of the English countryside than all the generations before us since Julius
Caesar came, shall need in our turn all the indulgence
of posterity. We shall be fortunate indeed, if we are
judged to have added half as much as the Victorians
to the beauty of English literature. For there were
giants in those days; and their farewell has been
finely uttered by one of the greatest and the last and
most lovable of them all, Thomas Hardy himself.

> The bower we shrined to Tennyson,
>> Gentlemen,
> Is roof-wrecked; damps there drip upon
> Sagged seats, the creeper nails are rust,
> The spider is sole denizen;
> Even she who read those rhymes is dust,
>> Gentlemen.
>
> And ye, red-lipped and smooth-browed; list,
>> Gentlemen;
> Much there is waits you we have missed;
> Much lore we leave you worth the knowing,
> Much, much has lain outside our ken:
> Nay, rush not: time serves: we are going
>> Gentlemen.

SELECTED BIBLIOGRAPHY

This bare list is intended merely to suggest a few starting-points for further reading. Where there is more than one edition, the date of the latest is given. Unless otherwise stated, books were published in London.

A. GENERAL.

E. Legouis and L. Cazamian, *Histoire de la Littérature Anglaise*. Paris, 1924. (There is an English translation.)

O: Elton, *A Survey of English Literature, 1830–80*. 1920.

B. Ifor Evans, *English Poetry in the Later Nineteenth Century*. 1933.

G. K. Chesterton, *The Victorian Age in Literature*. 1913.

The Cambridge History of English Literature, vol. XIII. Cambridge, 1916.

The Cambridge Bibliography of English Literature. Cambridge, 1940.

B. INDIVIDUAL POETS.

1. TENNYSON.
   H. Nicolson, *Tennyson*. 1925.

2. BROWNING.
   G. K. Chesterton, *Browning*. 1903.
   W. C. De Vane, *A Browning Handbook*. 1937.
   W. H. Griffin and H. C. Minchin, *The Life of R. Browning*. 1938.

3. ARNOLD.
   H. W. Garrod, *Poetry and the Criticism of Life*. Oxford, 1931.
   H. F. Lowry, *The Letters of M. Arnold to A. M. Clough*. 1932.
   L. Trilling, *M. Arnold*. 1939.

SELECTED BIBLIOGRAPHY

C. B. Tinker and H. F. Lowry, *The Poetry of M. Arnold*. 1940.
E. K. Chambers, *M. Arnold*. Oxford, 1947.

4. CLOUGH.
J. I. Osborne, *Clough*. 1920.
G. Levy, *Clough*. 1938.

5. COVENTRY PATMORE.
Sir E. Gosse, *C. Patmore*. 1905.
D. C. Patmore, *Portrait of my Family*. 1935.

6–7. THE ROSSETTIS.
F. Winwar, *The Rossettis and their Circle*. Boston, 1933.
W. Gaunt, *The Pre-Raphaelite Tragedy*. 1942.
Max Beerbohm, *Rossetti and his Circle*. 1922.
V. Woolf, " I am Christina Rossetti ", in *The Common Reader* (second series). 1932.

8. MORRIS.
J. W. Mackail, *Life of William Morris*. 1901.
A. Clutton-Brock, *W. Morris*. 1914.
Paul Bloomfield, *W. Morris*. 1934.
G. H. Crow, *W. Morris, Designer*. 1934.

9. SWINBURNE.
Sir E. Gosse, *Life of Swinburne*. 1917.
P. de Reul, *L'Œuvre de Swinburne*. 1922.
G. Lafourcade, *Swinburne*. 1932.

10. HARDY.
F. E. Hardy, *Early Life of T. Hardy*, 1928; *Later Years of T. Hardy*, 1930.
A. McDowall, *T. Hardy*. 1931.
W. R. Rutland, *T. Hardy*. Oxford, 1938.
C. J. Weber, *Hardy of Wessex*. New York, 1940.
E. Blunden, *T. Hardy*. 1491.